GLOSTER
METEOR

M.J. Hardy

Foulis

Haynes

ISBN 0-85429-451-1

A FOULIS Aircraft Book

© **Winchmore Publishing
Services Ltd 1985**

Avro Vulcan (F436)
B29 Superfortress (F339)
Boeing 707 (F356)
De Havilland Mosquito (F422)
Harrier (F357)
Mikoyan-Gurevich MiG 21 (F439)
P51 Mustang (F423)
Phantom II (F376)
Sea King (F377)
SEPECAT Jaguar (F438)
Super Etendard (F378)
Tiger Moth (F421)
Grumman Bearcat F8F (F447)
Hawker Hunter (F448)
Douglas Dakota (F449)
Hercules (F450)
Bell Helicopter (F437)

Further titles in this series will be published at
regular intervals. For information on new titles
please contact your bookseller or write to the
publisher.

Published by:
Haynes Publishing Group
Sparkford, Yeovil,
Somerset BA22 7JJ

Haynes Publications Inc.
861 Lawrence Drive,
Newbury Park,
California 91320, USA

Produced by:
**Winchmore Publishing Services
Limited,**
40 Triton Square,
London NW1 3HG

Printed in England

Contents

Genesis   4

The Meteor Prototypes   12

The Meteor enters service   15

The Meteor F.III   25

Ejector seat trials   29

Breaking the world speed record   31

The Meteor F.IV   34

The Meteor Trainer   37

The Meteor Test-Beds   41

The Meteor F. 8   44

The Meteor F. 8 overseas   46

Photo Recce and target drone variants   49

The Night Fighters   51

Specifications   55

Genesis

The Gloster Meteor was notable as being the first British jet aircraft to go into large-scale quantity production, as well as being the only Allied jet fighter actually to see combat service in World War II. It had two engines because, when design work began, no single jet engine then available or in prospect gave enough power to produce the required speed. Even then, the prototypes and the first production Meteor F.Is were only marginally faster than the fastest piston-engined fighters at the end of the war. Unusually for so significant a development, jet propulsion in this country had been brought to the stage of practical fruition by individuals – led by the genius of Frank Whittle – and firms who were largely outside the established aero-engine industry. This meant that Whittle and his team, working on a shoestring budget, had to go for the simplest possible jet engine of centrifugal-flow type, with a single-stage turbine. This simple approach paid great dividends in terms of reliability and growth potential; the Welland I in the Meteor F.I was cleared for 180 hours between overhauls in May 1944, whereas the German turbojets with their more complicated axial-flow compressors suffered severely from lack of reliability, and a much shorter life between overhauls.

With the more powerful Derwent 5 in the Meteor F.4, the basic airframe's full potentialities could be realised, and it twice broke the World's Absolute Air Speed Record. The Meteor also played an important part in the development of the Martin-Baker ejector seat, in-flight refuelling trials and as an engine test bed, test-flying the world's first turboprop and the first British reheat installation. Although outclassed by swept-wing types by the early 1950s, it enjoyed a new lease of life as a two-seat night fighter, not finally retiring from RAF first-line service until August 1961.

'I thought there was just a bare chance that something might come of it,' recalled Air Commodore Frank Whittle of his early ideas for jet propulsion. He was delivering the first James Clayton Lecture to the Institution of Mechanical Engineers, given in October 1945, in which he recounted the early history of jet engine development in Britain. The words quoted above were his feelings when, in May 1935, while an RAF Engineer Officer at Cambridge taking the Tripos Course, he was approached by two ex-RAF officers invalided out of the Service, R. D. Williams and J. C. B. Tinling, with a view to getting something started in the field of jet design and construction. This led to the formation of Power Jets Ltd in March 1936, but initially Whittle regarded Williams and Tinling as 'extremely optimistic'.

He had first started thinking about this general subject in 1928, while in his fourth term as a Flight Cadet at the RAF College, Cranwell. Each term the cadets had to write a science thesis, and that term Whittle chose as his subject future developments in aircraft, discussing amongst other things the possibilities of jet propulsion and of gas turbines. It was not until 18 months later, while on an Instructors' Course at the Central Flying School, Wittering, that he conceived the idea of using a gas turbine *for* jet propulsion, and it was this bringing together of the two principles that was Whittle's distinctive contribution in this field.

The two 'Vintage Pair' Meteor T.7s, WA669 and WF791 which, with Vampire T.11 XH304 in the background, formed the Central Flying School's Historic Aircraft Flight. WF791 reached the end of her fatigue life shortly after this photo was taken in April 1984, but WA669 continues to fly. This view shows well the distinctive fin and rudder shape.

Whittle took out his first patent, No 347206, on 16 January 1930 and tried to interest the Air Ministry and various firms in industry in the basic idea – but without success. The practical difficulties were considered too great, and the depression years of the 1930s were not the best time for such an advanced concept. For a time Whittle gave up hope of getting his idea to the practical stage, and allowed the original patent to lapse through failure to pay the renewal fee, although he continued to do paper work on the project at intervals. This was the situation when he met Williams and Tinling at Cambridge; they formed Power Jets Ltd with the help of investment bankers O.T. Falk and Partners, with an initial capital of £2,000. The Air Ministry was a shareholder from the start, in that a proportion of the shares allotted to Whittle was held in trust for it.

Even before Power Jets Ltd was formed, Whittle had started work on the design of an experimental engine, and O.T. Falk and Partners placed an order with the British Thomson-Houston Co Ltd (BTH), makers of industrial turbines, for engineering and design work in accordance with Whittle's requirements. This was followed in June 1936 by an order from Power Jets to BTH for the manufacture of the engine, except for the combustion chamber. This engine was based on a design for flight, but was not intended for flight and was kept very simple, having a single-stage centrifugal compressor with bilateral intakes, driven by a single-stage turbine directly coupled to it, and with just a single combustion chamber. Simple though the engine was, Whittle was going beyond all previous experience in his design objectives for these components, aiming at a pressure ratio of about 4:1 (when a ratio of 2½:1 had not been exceeded with a similar compressor), a power output of over 3,000 shp from a turbine

wheel of about 16½ in (42 cm) outside diameter, and a combustion intensity far beyond anything previously attempted. Combustion was the most difficult and least-known area, and here Whittle enlisted the aid of a specialist oil-burner firm, Laidlaw, Drew and Co, who designed and made the combustion chamber for the first engine, which was known as the 'U'.

This began test running on 12 April 1937, and tests continued intermittently until 23 August that year. In those early days, test facilities were primitive by today's standards, and there were several alarming occasions when uncontrolled acceleration of the engine up to as much as around 9,000 rpm occurred, leading the people monitoring the test to take cover in case the compressor burst or the turbine disintegrated. As Whittle wryly recalled in his James Clayton lecture, 'In the early days the individuals in the vicinity did more running than the engine.' The first engine was in fact rebuilt three times before finally being wrecked by turbine disc failure on 22 February 1941, and financial stringencies meant that parts which should really have been scrapped had to be used in reconstruction. But gradually the combustion problem – the most difficult area of all – came closer to a satisfactory solution, and by the summer of 1939, just before the start of World War II, the Air Ministry came to accept that Power Jets had here the basis for a practicable flight engine. A contract was awarded to the firm for such an engine, known as the Whittle W.1, and design drawings and manufacture of this were subcontracted by Power Jets to BTH, whose engineers, as well as a few from Power Jets and Whittle himself, made up the design team. Whittle had for some time now been provided with an office in the BTH works and had enjoyed access at all times to BTH's Chief Turbine Engineer and his colleagues, which

helped his work along greatly.

A contract was awarded to the Gloster Aircraft Co Ltd on 3 February 1940 for two prototypes of an aeroplane to Specification E.28/39 to flight-test the Whittle W.I engine, which specification also called for provision for four 0.303-in (7.7-mm) Browning machine-guns for the aircraft's possible use as a fighter. At about the same time, the Air Ministry took several important decisions based on the assumption that there was now a good chance of getting jet-propelled fighters into production in time to be used in the war. Firstly, Power Jets were authorised to go ahead with a more advanced jet engine, the Whittle W.2. Secondly it was decided that Power Jets would henceforth be a research and development organisation, and were to supply other firms engaged in jet engine work with all necessary drawings or other information necessary for their work. Thirdly, Specification F.9/40 was issued to cover the Gloster proposals for a single-seat twin-jet fighter which was later to be known as the Meteor. Fourthly, direct contracts were placed with BTH and several other firms for the development and manufacture of jet engines.

Power Jets worked closely with Gloster while the E.28/39 was being designed; this emerged as a small conventional low-wing monoplane of only 29 ft (8.84 m) span and 25 ft 3¾ in (7.72 m) length. The engine was buried in the fuselage between the wings and supplied with air through a bifurcated intake duct from the nose, exhausting through a tailpipe running down the rear fuselage. This type of nose intake duct (also known as a pitot entry) did pose some problems for aircraft featuring it; it took up a lot of internal fuselage space that might have been occupied by guns, radar or other equipment, there were friction losses in the duct and the cockpit was subject to excessive cooling by the air being

1 Starboard detachable wingtip
2 Starboard navigation light
3 Starboard recognition light
4 Starboard aileron
5 Aileron balance tab
6 Aileron mass balance weights
7 Aileron control coupling
8 Aileron torque shaft
9 Chain sprocket
10 Cross-over control runs
11 Front spar
12 Rear spar
13 Aileron (inboard) mass balance
14 Nacelle detachable tail section
15 Jet pipe exhaust
16 Internal stabilising struts
17 Rear spar "spectacle" frame
18 Fire extinguishing spray ring
19 Main engine mounting frame
20 Engine access panel(s)
21 Nacelle nose structure
22 Intake internal leading-edge shroud
23 Starboard engine intake
24 Windscreen de-icing spray pipe
25 Reflector gunsight
26 Cellular glass bullet-proof
   windscreen
27 Aft-sliding cockpit canopy

28 Demolition incendiary (cockpit
   starboard wall)
29 RPM indicators (left and right of
   gunsight)
30 Pilot's seat
31 Forward fuselage top deflector skin
32 Gun wobble button
33 Control column grip
34 Main instrument panel

35 Nosewheel armoured bulkhead
36 Nose release catches (10)
37 Nosewheel jack bulkhead housing/
   attachment

38 Nose ballast weight location
39 Nosewheel mounting frames
40 Radius rod (link and jack omitted)
41 Nosewheel pivot bearings
42 Shimmy-damper/self-centering strut
43 Gun camera
44 Camera access
45 Aperture
46 Nose cone
47 Cabin cold-air intake
48 Nosewheel leg door
49 Picketing rings
50 Tension shock absorber
51 Pivot bracket
52 Mudguard
53 Torque strut
54 Door hoop
55 Wheel fork
56 Retractable nosewheel
57 Nosewheel doors
58 Port cannon trough fairings
59 Nosewheel cover
60 Intermediate diaphragm
61 Blast tubes
62 Gun front mounting rails
63 Pilot's seat pan
64 Emergency crowbar
65 Canopy de-misting silica gel cylinder
66 Bullet-proof glass rear-view cut-outs
67 Canopy track
68 Seat bulkhead
69 Entry step
70 Link ejection chutes
71 Case ejection chutes
72 20-mm Hispano Mk III cannon
73 Belt fed mechanism
74 Ammunition feed necks
75 Ammunition tanks
76 Aft glazing (magazine bay top door)
77 Loading ramp
78 Front spar bulkhead
79 Oxygen bottles (2)

80 Front spar carry-through
81 Tank bearer frames
82 Rear spar carry-through
83 Self-sealing (twin compartment)
   main fuel tank, capacity 165 Imp gal
   (750 l) in each half
84 Fuel connector pipe
85 Return pipe
86 Drain pipes
87 Fuel filler caps
88 Tank doors (2)

89 T.R. 1143 serial mast
90 Rear spar bulkhead (plywood face)
91 Aerial support frame
92 R.3121 (or B.C.966A) IFF installation
93 Tab control cables
94 Amplifier
95 Fire extinguisher bottles (2)
96 Elevator torque shaft
97 T.R.1143 transmitter/receiver radio
   installation
98 Pneumatic system filter
99 Pneumatic system (compressed) air
   cylinders
100 Tab cable fairlead

101 Elevator control cable
102 Top longeron
103 Fuselage frame
104 IFF aerial
105 DR compass master unit
106 Rudder cables
107 Starboard lower longeron
108 Cable access panels (port and
    starboard)
109 Tail section joint
110 Rudder linkage
111 Tail ballast weight location
112 Fin spar/fuselage frame
113 Rudder tab control
114 Fin structure
115 Torpedo fairing

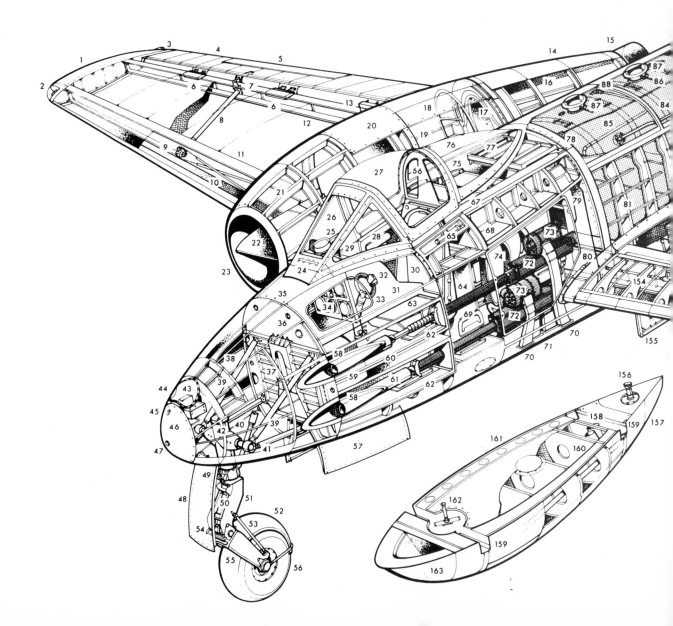

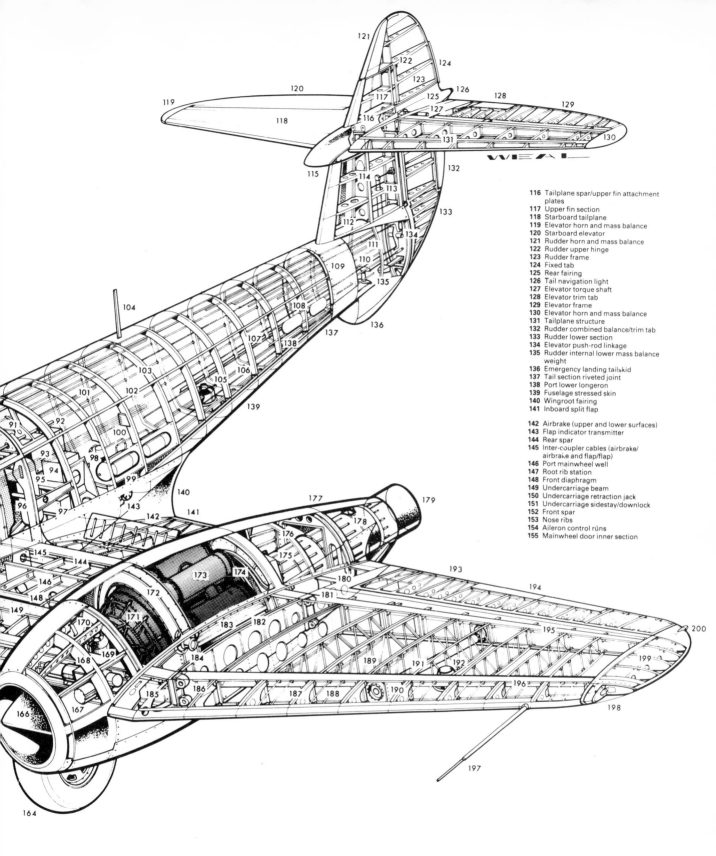

116 Tailplane spar/upper fin attachment plates
117 Upper fin section
118 Starboard tailplane
119 Elevator horn and mass balance
120 Starboard elevator
121 Rudder horn and mass balance
122 Rudder upper hinge
123 Rudder frame
124 Fixed tab
125 Rear fairing
126 Tail navigation light
127 Elevator torque shaft
128 Elevator trim tab
129 Elevator frame
130 Elevator horn and mass balance
131 Tailplane structure
132 Rudder combined balance/trim tab
133 Rudder lower section
134 Elevator push-rod linkage
135 Rudder internal lower mass balance weight
136 Emergency landing tailskid
137 Tail section riveted joint
138 Port lower longeron
139 Fuselage stressed skin
140 Wingroot fairing
141 Inboard split flap

142 Airbrake (upper and lower surfaces)
143 Flap indicator transmitter
144 Rear spar
145 Inter-coupler cables (airbrake/ airbrake and flap/flap)
146 Port mainwheel well
147 Root rib station
148 Front diaphragm
149 Undercarriage beam
150 Undercarriage retraction jack
151 Undercarriage sidestay/downlock
152 Front spar
153 Nose ribs
154 Aileron control runs
155 Mainwheel door inner section

156 Ventral tank transfer pipe
157 Tank rear fairing
158 Filler stack pipes
159 Ventral tank attachment strap access doors
160 Anti-surge baffles
161 Fixed ventral fuel tank, capacity 105 Imp gal (477l)
162 Air pressure inlet
163 Tank front fairing
164 Port mainwheel
165 Starboard engine intake
166 Intake internal leading-edge shroud

167 Auxiliary gearbox drives (vacuum pump/generator)
168 Nacelle nose structure
169 Starter motor
170 Oil tank
171 Rolls-Royce W.2B/23C Welland I turbojet
172 Main engine mounting frame
173 Combustion chambers
174 Rear spar "spectacle" frame
175 Jet pipe thermo-coupling
176 Nacelle aft frames
177 Nacelle detachable tail section

178 Jet pipe suspension link
179 Jet pipe exhaust
180 Gap fairing tail section
181 Rear spar outer wing fixing
182 Outer wing rib No 1
183 Engine end rib
184 Engine mounting/removal trunnion
185 Gap fairing nose section
186 Front spar outer wing fixing
187 Nose ribs
188 Intermediate riblets
189 Wing ribs
190 Aileron drive chain sprocket

191 Aileron torque shaft
192 Retractable landing lamp
193 Port aileron
194 Aileron balance tab
195 Rear spar
196 Front spar
197 Pitot head
198 Port navigation light
199 Outer wing rib No 10/wingtip attachment
200 Port recognition light

Genesis

drawn in, to name only some of the 'snags'. Without a long engine and airscrew in front of him, the E.28/39's pilot enjoyed an excellent view, and the short nosewheel undercarriage embodied the Dowty levered suspension principle which was also applied to the Meteor's landing gear; the nosewheel retracted backwards and the main wheels turned to lie flat in the wing.

While the W.1 engine was being built, certain major components were considered on completion to be unairworthy; it was decided to use these, plus certain spare components made for the first 'U' experimental engine, to build an early edition of the W.1, not intended to be flown and known as the W.1X. This proved to be far in advance of the first 'U' experimental engine and, although not wholly satisfactory, certain modifications suggested by test running of the W.1X were incorporated into the W.1, which underwent a 25 hours' special category test to clear it for flight. The W.1X was installed in the prototype E.28/39 W4041/G for taxiing trials, carried out at Hucclecote on 7 April 1941 by Flt Lt P. E. G. 'Jerry' Sayer, during the course of which the aircraft actually left the ground for a short straight hop.

W4041/G was then fitted with the 860-lb (300-kg) s.t. (maximum take-off) W.1 engine and was transported by road to RAF Cranwell, where there was a longer runway. It was readied for flight by 14 May 1941, further taxiing trials being done that day. The actual first flight was made late the following evening by 'Jerry' Sayer and lasted 17 minutes, being entirely successful. This was the first-ever flight of a British jet aeroplane, and it was especially appropriate that it took place at Cranwell, where the young Whittle had first put down his thoughts on jet propulsion 12 years before. The W.1 in W4041/G had been cleared for 10 hours'

flying, and it proved to be sufficiently trouble-free to complete this initial period on 28 May without special incident, doing 17 flights totalling 10 hours 28 minutes. The W.1 engine in W4041/G ran 39 hours 57 minutes in all, including bench tests, taxiing trials and flying, and on being dismantled it was found to be in excellent condition.

Test flying was then transferred to Edgehill in Warwickshire, where flights recommenced on 4

Above: Close-up of the Meteor nosewheel which, like the main wheels, embodied the Dowty levered suspension principle pioneered in the Gloster E.28/39.

Top right: Each main wheel leg retracts inwards into a bay in the centre section behind two closed doors. The forward undercarriage jack compresses the main leg on retraction to reduce the space it occupies and enable it to fit in the wheel bay.

Bottom right: The 180-Imp gal (818-litre) ventral drop tank on one of the 'Vintage Pair' Meteor T.7s. Note retractable footsteps for the pilots projecting from lower fuselage.

Genesis

February 1942 with W4041/G re-engined with a 1,160-lb (526-kg) s.t. W.1A engine and fitted with a new high-speed wing of revised aerofoil section. The W.1A was similar to the W.1 but incorporated certain special features of the W.2 engine on which Power Jets were then working, and for which advanced testing was deemed desirable. The W.1A had been fitted in W4041/G on 7 January 1942 but there were some problems later with this powerplant and on one occasion the aircraft was slightly damaged. After 'Jerry' Sayer was unfortunately killed in another type of aircraft on 21 October 1942, flying was continued by Gloster test pilot Michael Daunt.

The success of W4041/G's initial flight tests in May 1941 gave a powerful boost to the whole British jet engine programme; the Ministry of Aircraft Production (MAP) made plans for production of the W.2 engine in its W.2B form as well as the F.9/40, which became the Meteor, and those firms already engaged in jet engine work stepped up the tempo of their activities. Among the latter was the Rover Company, which had been brought in by the Air Ministry in the early spring of 1940 to build the W.2 engine from drawings supplied by Power Jets. It was realised before this engine was completed that if certain design assumptions in respect of component efficiencies were not met, the penalties would be severe. This proved to be the case and the first W.2 was in fact a failure. It was developed through the W.2 Mk IV, which was built by BTH under sub-contract to Power Jets, to the W.2B which was designed by Power Jets with the first two examples being built by the Rover Co.

The W.2B was the prototype of the Rolls-Royce Welland, which powered the Meteor F.I; it formed the basis of the General Electric Type IA that powered the Bell XP-59A Airacomet, the first US jet

fighter. In the autumn of 1941 the MAP, to its credit, encouraged competitive developments of the same basic engine, allowing the Rover Co to go ahead with its own ideas for improving the W.2B's performance, so that this engine was developed along two main lines. The first of these was to the limits of the combustion chamber as originally conceived by Power Jets, and the second line of development was the 'straight-through' combustion system for the W.2B, developed by the Rover Co and later by Rolls-Royce. Air burned at the front of the combustion chamber expanded and flowed straight down it to the turbine blades, instead of, as in the earlier 'return flow' combustion system of Power Jets, being burnt at the opposite end of the chamber and then making a 180° change in direction through an 'elbow' in the chamber before reaching the turbine.

By redesigning the compressor casing and diffuser, thus raising the engine's surging speed and improving performance, Rover produced the W.2B/23, which Rolls-Royce put into production as the Welland I when they took over Rover's gas turbine work on 1 April 1943. In March 1942 Rover had run their prototype W.2B/26, which featured the 'straight-through' combustion system actually originated by Power Jets, but which the latter did not favour at that time although it appealed to Rover because it made manufacture easier. This engine served as the prototype of the Derwent I, which powered the Meteor F.III, and Rover did some of the early design work on the Derwent until Rolls-Royce took over and completed it. Rolls took over the Rover Co's Barnoldswick factory, and designated the Derwent the RB.37, the letters RB standing for Rolls Barnoldswick; this Rolls designation prefix has continued in use to this day for their jet engines, with the big RB.211 turbofan and the RB.199 for

the Tornado. Small production batches of the W.2 built by Power Jets were known as the W.2/500, which first ran in September 1942 and had slightly longer turbine blades than the W.2B, and the W.2/700.

The second prototype E.28/39 W4046/G, with a Rover-built W.2B of 1,200-lb (545-kg) s.t., made its first flight on 1 March 1943 in the hands of John Grierson – but its career was short-lived. On a flight from Farnborough on 30 July that year, it went into an inverted spin when the ailerons jammed at 37,000 ft (11,277 m), although the pilot, Sqn Ldr Davie, succeeded in bailing out at 33,000 ft (10,058 m).

W4041/G continued the test programme, being re-engined with a 1,700-lb (771-kg) s.t. Power Jets W.2/500, with which flying commenced in May 1943. At the end of that year, a new and improved W.2/500 of 1,760-lb (798-kg) s.t. was fitted, small endplate fins being added to the tailplane to increase the fin area and a jettisonable cockpit hood installed in place of the earlier one. Thus modified, W4041/G began flying again in April 1944; when these flight trials were completed, its flying days were over. It is now preserved for posterity in the Science Museum, South Kensington, London.

In addition to the E.28/39, which was sometimes known as the Pioneer (although the name never caught on), three Wellington B.IIs were used as jet engine test beds. These were W5518/G, fitted with a Rover-built W.2B/23 in the tail in place of the gun turret, first flying with this engine in August 1942, and W5389, which was fitted with a Derwent I similarly mounted. These two were used by Rolls-Royce, while Wellington B.II Z5870/G was fitted with a W.2/700 of 2,000-lb (908-kg) s.t. in the extreme tail for use by Power Jets. It first flew with this engine in July 1942; later, a Rover-built W.2B was fitted, and the piston engines fitted were

The Meteor F.I seen here had Rolls-Royce Welland I turbojets and a sideways-opening cockpit canopy instead of the rearward-sliding one of later marks. This mark began to equip No 616 Squadron on 12 July 1944; the Meteor was the only Allied jet to see action in the war.

Merlin Xs, and later Merlin XXs. W5389 and W5518/G were hybrid Wellingtons, having the B.II's fuselage and the wings of the high-altitude Wellington VI, with Merlin 62 engines for testing at greater heights.

The Meteor Prototypes

The progress made with the Whittle W.1 engine before the E.28/39's first flight, and the promise of other jet engines then being planned, led to an increasingly confident view that it was only a matter of time before a jet engine satisfactory and reliable enough for a production fighter would emerge. By mid-1940 design work was beginning at the Gloster Aircraft Co Ltd under George Carter on just such a single-seat fighter. It had two turbojets because no single jet engine then available or in prospect gave enough power to produce the required speed. In November 1940 Gloster's proposals for the twin-jet fighter were given the go-ahead by the Air Ministry and Specification F.9/40 was written around them. On 7 February 1941, no less than 12 prototypes of what was to be known as the Meteor were ordered (DG202-DG213), although in the event the last four of these (DG210-DG213) were cancelled.

In September of that year there was sufficient confidence in the basic Gloster F.9/40 design, and in British jet engine development generally, for the MAP to place an initial production order for 20 Meteor F.Is (EE210-EE229), 18 months before the first flight by an F.9/40 prototype. The type was originally named Thunderbolt, but this was changed to Meteor in March 1942 when the Republic P-47 Thunderbolt appeared in the States.

The F.9/40 was of quite conventional appearance, with an unswept low aspect ratio wing of thin laminar-flow section; this did not hold any fuel, which was carried in a tank in the centre fuselage. In the Meteor F.4, this tank's capacity was 325 Imp gallons (1,478 litres). The engines were centrally mounted rather than underslung, as the centrifugal-flow turbojets that powered all but one of the F.9/40 prototypes and production Meteors were short enough to fit neatly between the wing spars. This did give rise to a structural design problem in that the rear spar had to be enlarged to a 'banjo' shape to allow the jet pipe to pass through it; intake air passed over and under the front spar before reaching the compressor. The pilot was seated well forward, where he had an outstanding view, and the F.9/40 was the first single-seat fighter of British design with a nosewheel undercarriage. The nosewheel retracted backwards and the main wheels inwards, these being fitted with a shortening device to reduce the space they occupied when retracted.

The Meteor had been planned to be built in sub-assembly units in widely-dispersed factories, and to this end its structure was designed to break down into easily managed and transportable units; this made it especially easy to transport and repair in service. The fuselage was divided into three major units – a nose, centre and rear section – while the wing was made up of the centre-section and two outer panels. Special attention was paid to ease of maintenance, the complete top half of each engine cowling between the spars being detachable, and large access doors were provided for the guns and ammunition.

Armament was four 20-mm Hispano Mk II cannon mounted on

each side of the cockpit between the main fuselage diaphragm members and the outer skin; the guns were low enough for the pilot to be unaffected by flash when they were fired, and yet were high enough to prevent nosing down when firing. The original F.9/40 design featured six 20-mm cannon, the two extra guns being situated under the cabin floor, but these were deleted on the grounds of accessibility, especially if they were jammed. They were in fact fitted solely to one of the F.9/40 prototypes but were fired only on the ground. Their deletion led to a growing problem of tail heaviness, and the need for more and more ballast in the nose, as the type was developed and modifications such as the lengthened nacelles were introduced. The Meteor F.4 had to carry up to 1,095 lb (497 kg) of lead ballast on the nose bulkhead and elsewhere in order to keep the centre of gravity within limits. This problem was cured in the Meteor F.8 by lengthening the forward fuselage by 30 in (76 cm) to accommodate an extra fuel tank. Cases and links from the guns were ejected through small chutes in the bottom fuselage skin, and there was a G.45B cine camera in

the extreme nose to record the results of firing.

The first prototype F.9/40 DG202 was fitted with Rover-built W.2Bs rated at only 1,000-lb (454-kg) s.t. each and, because of their low power, due to a series of difficulties, only taxiing trials were possible at first. These started at Newmarket Heath on 10 July 1942, but delays in developing the W.2B up to its full power of 1,800-lb (816-kg) s.t. meant that the first F.9/40 to fly was powered by Halford H.1 turbojets. DG202 underwent further taxiing trials and did not fly until June 1943, later serving Rolls-Royce as a test bed. DG206 was the Halford H.1-powered prototype, with a pair of these centrifugal flow engines each rated at 1,500-lb (680-kg) s.t. The H.1 was designed by Major Frank B. Halford, who had been brought into the turbine field in January 1941 by Sir Henry Tizard and had a long line of famous British aero engines to his credit. These included the Cirrus for the first de Havilland D.H.60 Moth lightplane, which led to the Gipsy range for the Moth and other light aircraft. Halford also designed the Rapier and Dagger for Napier's, as well as the Sabre that powered the Typhoon. Design of the H.1 started in April 1941, and on 13 April 1942 the prototype H.1 made its first test run on its special test bed at Hatfield, sentries with tommy guns surrounding the building for security reasons. Such rapid construction was made possible by an elegantly simple design, with a single-sided compressor (instead of the double-sided ones of the Whittle and Rolls-Royce engines) and 'straight-through' combustion, with a single-stage turbine.

Because the de Havilland Vampire prototype was not yet ready, the first flight of the H.1 took place in F.9/40 DG206. Piloted on

5 March 1943 by Gloster test pilot Michael Daunt from Cranwell, this was also the first flight of the F.9/40. The H.1 went into production as the de Havilland Goblin for the Vampire; a proposed production version of the H.1-engined F.90/40 would have been the Meteor F.II, but this was not built, partly to reserve Goblin production for the Vampire. A second F.9/40, DG207, was also fitted with these engines with higher thrust – 2,700-lb (1,225-kg) s.t., the installation of which required some modifications to the wing – and, with DG206, was used as a test-bed for the Goblin. On one occasion Michael Daunt had his head and shoulders in an F.9/40 Goblin intake when ground running started, and only prompt action on the throttle lever saved him from death or serious injury. On 30 October 1943 a Halford H.1 turbojet left for Prestwick on a lorry en route to Lockheed at Burbank, California, for installation in the prototype XF-80 Shooting Star. It was loaded on to a C-54 Skymaster at Prestwick for trans-shipment at New York, and the lorry was given special permission to use undimmed headlights, although the blackout was then in force. The company bearing Major Halford's name worked in close collaboration with de Havilland on the H.1's design, and on 1 February 1944 became part of the DH enterprise when the de Havilland Engine Co Ltd was formed to take over the old DH Engine Division. Halford himself was appointed Chairman and Technical Director of the new company.

The next F.9/40 prototype to make its first flight after the H.1-powered DG206 was DG202, previously mentioned. It was followed by DG205/G, which took to the air at Barford St John, near Banbury in Oxfordshire, on 24 July 1943 and was powered by 1,400-lb (635-kg) s.t. Rolls-Royce W.2B/23 engines, which entered production as the Welland I. For this prototype's second flight, a new

Left: The Gloster F.9/40 first prototype of the Meteor, DG202/G, was fitted with two Rover-built W.2B turbojets of only 1,000 lb (454 kg) s.t. each, with which it began taxiing trials on 10 July 1942.

pair of W.2B/23s, developing 1,600-lb (726-kg) s.t. each, were fitted. The seventh prototype, DG208, also had W.2B/23 engines, first flying on 20 January 1944; this F.9/40 also had a rudder of increased area and was fitted with air brakes on the wings, which were to be a feature of production aircraft. The second prototype DG203 first flew in November 1943 with two 1,650-lb (748-kg) s.t. Power Jets W.2/500 engines, and in April 1944 this was fitted with 2,000-lb (907-kg) s.t. Power Jets W.2/700 turbojets.

The third prototype DG204/G was fitted with two 1800-lb (816-kg) s.t. Metrovick F.2/1 axial-flow jet engines, and made its first flight on 13 November 1943 at Farnborough. This was the first British aircraft to fly powered by turbojets with an axial-flow compressor, and because the F2/1 was longer than the centrifugal-flow engines fitted to other F.9/40s, and would not fit between the main spars, the engines were underslung from the wings like the Messerschmitt Me 262's. The Metropolitan-Vickers Electrical Co Ltd, or Metrovick, had been associated with the design of an airscrew-driving gas turbine based on the preliminary theoretical and research work into axial-flow compressors begun by Dr A. A. Griffith (later of Rolls-Royce) at the RAE as far back as 1926. By the outbreak of war, several experimental axial-flow compressors had undergone ground-running at the RAE and elsewhere with some success.

As early as November 1929 Dr Griffith, in a technical paper, examined the possibilities of an airscrew-driving turbine based on a contra-rotating, contra-flow principle and concluded that such an engine could be lighter, smaller and more efficient than piston engines. In March 1937, Mr Hayne Constant of the RAE, in a paper on a similar type of turboprop, reached similar conclusions and Metrovick collaborated with the

RAE on design studies of several layouts of such an engine. One of these, known as the B.10, was built and ran very successfully in December 1940, foreshadowing present-day engines in having low- and high-pressure axial compressors driving low- and high-pressure turbines. Metrovick started design of the axial-flow F.2 in July 1940, with preliminary design being done under Mr Hayne Constant at the RAE. The F.2 had a nine-stage axial-flow compressor, a single annular combustion chamber and a two-stage turbine. Bench testing of the F.2 began in December 1941 and after modifications it passed a special category 25-hour test in November 1942. The F.2 was later developed into the F.2/4 Beryl, which powered the little Saunders-Roe SR/A1 flying boat fighter, and was also test-flown in Meteor F.4 RA490. A higher-powered development of this, known as the Sapphire, was begun but further development and production of this engine was taken over in 1948 by Armstrong Siddeley Motors Ltd when Metrovick decided to pull out of the jet engine field. By the late 1950s the axial-flow engine had become the dominant type of turbojet, partly because beyond about 7,500-lb (3402-kg) s.t. the centrifugal type's compressor diameter became too large even for wing root or fuselage installations.

The eighth F.9/40 prototype DG209 first flew on 18 April 1944 with two 2,000-lb (907-kg) s.t. RB.37 Derwent Is, being the first to have the type of engine that was to power most production Meteors. As related in the previous chapter, Rover had run their W.2B/26 development of the W.2B with 'straight-through' combustion and this served as the prototype of the Derwent I, Rolls-Royce taking over and completing design work on this engine when they took over Rover's gas turbine work on 1 April 1943. Whereas the Welland I, the production version of the W.2B/23,

had the Power Jets 'reverse flow' combustion system, the Derwent I had the 'straight-through' type of combustion pioneered by Rover. Otherwise the Derwent had the same overall and compressor diameters as the Welland, and was generally similar, with a higher thrust of 2,000-lb (907-kg) s.t. with a weight increase of only 70 lb (32 kg). In the Derwent I, air left the tip of the compressor at a speed of 1,380 ft/second, and reached each of the 10 radially-disposed combustion chambers at a pressure of 42 lb/sq in; maximum permissible jet pipe temperature for continuous cruising was 600°C. The thrust-to-weight ratio of Meteor engines improved from 1.86 for the Welland I to 2.08 for the Derwent I, and 2.78 for the Derwent V that powered the Meteor F.IV.

The fourth F.9/40 prototype DG205/G was flown by Boscombe Down test pilots on 28 and 29 February 1944; this had the 1,600-lb (726-kg) s.t. W.2B/23 engines. A. & A.E.E. Report No. 317 of 31 March 1944 on tests of this F.9/40 concluded that it was easy to fly, quiet and pleasantly absent of vibration and fumes.

The starting and use of the engines was simple, and taxiing straightforward, but throttle response was much slower than piston-engined types; there was no take-off swing but initial rate of climb was poor. There was complete freedom from engine noise but aerodynamic noise at higher speeds was appreciable; the lack of vibration made the pilot more aware of 'bumps' in flight. A serious disadvantage, especially in a baulked landing, was the 10-second restriction on the minimum time for opening up from idling to maximum r.p.m., and removal of this restriction was recommended in the report. Also recommended was a repositioning of the fuel and throttle controls and some instruments, and a slight tilting back of the pilot's seat.

The Meteor enters service

The F.9/40 went into production as the G.41A Meteor F.I with 1,700-lb (771-kg) s.t. Rolls-Royce Welland I turbojets. This initial version also differed from the Meteor F.III in having a sideways-opening clear-view cockpit canopy instead of a rearward-sliding one, and slightly less fuel capacity. EE210, the first production aircraft, made its maiden flight on 12 January 1944 and was later sent to the United States in exchange for the Bell YP-59A Airacomet 42-108773 which had been supplied to the RAF for evaluation as RJ362/G and which first flew in this country at Moreton Valence in September 1943. The RAF was unwilling to put the Meteor into squadron service until a reasonable engine-overhaul life had been achieved, and in May 1944 the Welland I in the Meteor F.I was cleared for 180 hours between overhauls. At the same time it also passed a 500-hour type test, and had passed a similar 100-hour test in April 1943, when Rolls-Royce took over the Rover Co's work.

This contrasted admirably with the Junkers Jumo 004B turbojets of the Messerschmitt Me 262, which could do only about 25 hours between overhauls and had had to be 'frozen' for assembly line production in June 1944 in an insufficiently developed state. Compressor reliability of that engine suffered from a shortage of the nickel and chrome needed for the turbine blades of the eight-stage axial-flow compressor, and there were continual problems with the fuel flow, so that engine failures with the Me 262 were frequent, often resulting in fatal crashes. In terms of both fuel consumption and power-to-weight ratio, the German BMW 003 and Jumo 004 turbojets compared unfavourably with the contemporary British engines, and in the closing stages of the war the Luftwaffe was having to take delivery of jet engines that would not have been acceptable to the RAF or the USAAF.

The first Meteor squadron was No. 616, which had been formed at Doncaster in November 1938 as No.616 (South Yorkshire) Sqn of the Auxiliary Air Force, and was flying Spitfire H.F.VIIs on offensive sweeps over France from Culmhead, Somerset, when the first Meteor F.I EE219 was delivered to it on 12 July 1944. On 21 July the squadron moved to Manston in Kent, receiving more Meteors two days later to make up a detached flight of seven aircraft. It had originally been intended that the squadron should work up for high-altitude air combat, but instead it began operating 'Diver' patrols against the Fieseler Fi 103 or V-1 flying bombs then appearing over southern England, flying the first 'Diver' patrol on 27 July. On 4 August Flying Officer Dean, in Meteor F.I EE216, made the first confirmed 'kill' of a V-1 near Tonbridge by formating on it at 365 mph (587 km/h) after his guns had jammed and turning it over with his wing tip. Flying Officer Roger shot down a second V-1 near Tenterden on the same day, using conventional gunfire; there was some trouble in firing the Meteor's guns at first but this was later rectified. Dean's V-1 was the first enemy aircraft to be destroyed by a British jet fighter, and the Meteor was the only Allied jet aircraft actually to see action in World War II.

By the end of August, No. 616 had converted entirely to Meteor F.Is and these had destroyed 13 V-1 flying bombs by the time the Germans had been driven out of the Pas de Calais area. With Me 262s appearing more and more often to intercept Allied bombers, No. 616 prepared for operations on the Continent. During October four Meteor F.Is were detached to Debden in Suffolk to participate in an exercise with the USAAF 2nd Bombardment Division and the 65th Fighter Wing to evolve tactics suitable for use against the Me 262s and rocket-powered Me 163 Komets. The Meteors were employed in making simulated attacks on the P-51 Mustangs and P-47 Thunderbolts escorting the American bombers. On 17 January 1945 the squadron moved to Colerne in Wiltshire and three days later one flight of Meteors joined 84 Group of the 2nd Tactical Air Force at Melsbroek airfield near Brussels. These were F.IIIs, the first of which had been delivered to No. 616 at Manston on 18 December 1944, and during January this new mark replaced the F.Is, which equipped only No. 616 Squadron.

Several Meteor F.Is were used experimentally, EE221/G being fitted with Power Jets W.2/700 engines, as was Meteor F.III EE249/G, which also had a pressurised cockpit and several other modifications. The third production F.I EE212/G later featured a non-standard tail unit and was Welland-powered; in its original form it was flown by A.&A.E.E. pilots between September and November 1944. The resulting Boscombe Down Report No.817 of 23 May 1945 considered it easy and pleasant to fly, with very good longitudinal stability, although some directional oscillation was apparent. The short engine nacelles caused buffeting at comparatively low Mach numbers, and this was later to be rectified by the lengthened nacelles fitted to the last 30 Meteor F.IIIs. Take-off and climb were found to be poor; a similar criticism had been made of the F.9/40 DG205/G when flown by Boscombe Down pilots, but this was largely due to the low power of the engines then fitted and the deficiency disappeared when more power became available.

Meteor F.I EE227, after a spell of squadron service with No. 616 coded YQ-Y, was converted into

15

the world's first turboprop-powered aeroplane when fitted with a pair of Derwent Is modified to drive 7 ft 11 in (2.41 m) diameter five-blade Rotol airscrews, through reduction gearing, this engine being known as the Trent and developing 750 s.h.p. plus 1,000 lb (453 kg) s.t. EE227 first flew with Trents on 20 September 1945 at Church Broughton in the hands of Mr Eric Greenwood, and it had a longer-stroke undercarriage to give adequate airscrew tip clearance, which was 11 in (28 cm), and two small endplate fins on the tailplane to increase the fin area. With Trents, EE227's maximum speed was 470 mph (756 km/h). Several Derwents were modified into Trents but this turboprop was not put into production. As related in the previous chapter, Dr A. A. Griffith had examined the possibilities of an airscrew-driving turbine in a technical paper as early as November 1929, and an experimental turbo-compressor very much as suggested by Dr Griffith was later designed at the RAE and built by Armstrong Siddeley Motors. It made test runs at the RAE in 1940, and although its performance proved to be indifferent, the fact that it ran at all was a vindication of the original theory behind it. An intriguing revelation about the Trent-Meteor was made in a lecture not long after the war by a test pilot who had flown it. He had found it possible to stop the five-blade airscrew rotating, after the throttle was closed down on the ground, simply by pressing his leather-gloved hands against the airscrew spinner, the smoothness of the gas turbine enabling it to be stopped in a manner that would have been impossible with a piston engine.

Also important historically, but not nearly as well-known as the Trent-Meteor, was Meteor F.I EE215 which in 1944 became the first British jet to have reheat. The jet from a turbine contains quantities of unburnt oxygen, which can be reheated to produce

extra thrust temporarily by burning additional fuel in it. This is inefficient thermodynamically, and expensive on fuel, but can be justified by the extra thrust made available for bursts of high speed, or for take-off. Power Jets carried out the first experiments in boosting thrust with ammonia, an addition of 6.15 per cent by weight to the air in a W.1 Mk III engine on the test bed giving a 28 per cent thrust increase; on the W.2B, an addition of 4.4 per cent of ammonia gave a thrust increase of 22.4 per cent. Methyl chloride was also tried, without success, but water injection was much more promising, an injection of 102 lb/minute on a W.2/700 producing a thrust increase of 18 per cent.

By burning 30 per cent, 70 per cent and 100 per cent more fuel in a W.2B/23, static thrust increases of 5 per cent, 10.8 per cent and 16 per cent respectively were

obtained, and it was estimated that at 500 mph (805 km/h) this would produce a thrust gain of up to 27.5 per cent with 100 per cent more fuel. The use of reheat also demanded a variable-area jet nozzle and, after several types had been considered in early experiments, a 'caliper' type of variable jet nozzle was found to be the best. Segments shaped like caliper blades reduced the nozzle's area progressively, in much the same way as a camera lens when the aperture is stopped down. It was to be some years before reheat or afterburning became a regular feature of military aircraft partly because of the difficulty of producing a satisfactory variable-area nozzle, and also because there was no point in 'going for the burn' (to use aerobics parlance) when the early post-war jet engines gave much higher speeds than piston engines could.

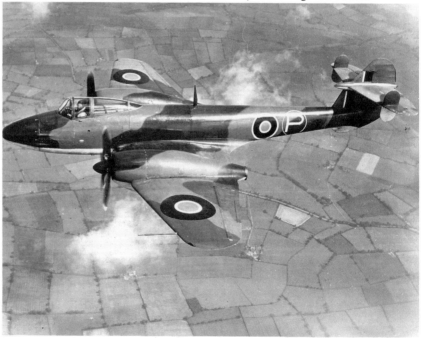

Above: Meteor F.I EE227 became the world's first turboprop-powered aeroplane when fitted with two Rolls-Royce Trents driving five-blade Rotol airscrews. The Trent was just a Derwent I modified to drive these 7 ft 11 in (2.41 m) diameter Rotol props.

Right: the Meteor T.7s WA669 and WF791 in formation with Vampire T.11 XH304 represent Training Command first-line equipment of the early and mid 1950s. All three carry the trainer markings of that period, being silver all over with yellow bands around the outer wings and rear fuselage.

Left: The RAF's last two Meteor T.7s, WA669 and WF791, from RAF Leeming, Yorkshire, seen in April 1984 over a cu-nim background. WF791 has now reached the end of its fatigue life and has been replaced by WA669.

Far left: This ground shot of one of the 'Vintage Pair' Meteor T.7s shows the 180-imp gal (818-litre) ventral drop tank.

Below: Another view of the Central Flying School 'Vintage Pair' Meteor T.7s, WA669 and WF791, in formation over cu-nim clouds.

Right: The all-yellow Meteor T.7 SE-CAS (ex-WF833) was delivered to the Swedish firm Svensk Flygtjänst AB in July 1955 for use as a target tug.

Left: The Gloster E.28/39 prototype W4041/G suspended from the roof of the Science Museum, South Kensington.

Bottom left: The Gloster F.9/40 Meteor first prototype DG202/G, powered by two Rover-built W.2B turbojets, is now preserved in the RAF Museum at Hendon. It has the yellow undersurfaces and prototype Ⓟ applied in wartime to prototypes and experimental aircraft.

Below: The yellow undersurfaces with black diagonal stripes reveal VZ567 seen here as a T.T.8 target tug conversion of a Meteor F.8; she belonged to No 229 OCU.

Bottom: Meteor N.F.11 WD790 is the last of this mark that is still flying with the RAF and is used by the Royal Signals and Radar Establishment at Pershore to flight test a new advanced radar.

Above left: Meteor F.8 WK991 bears the red and white checkerboard markings of No 56 Sqn, and is seen here at Duxford.

Above: Meteor F.8 "S" of No 615 (County of Surrey) Sqn has a white fin and rudder with two horizontal black zigzag flashes across it; note absence of fin flash.

Left: A77-875 seen here is one of 97 Meteor F.8s supplied to the Royal Australian Air Force; they were used to good effect by No 77 Sqn in the Korean campaign, and later equipped two squadrons of the Citizen Air Force.

Below: The Meteor N.F.(T) 14 was used to give jet experience to navigators under training until replaced by the Dominie jet from 1965. WS807 seen here was one of this variant used by No 1 Air Navigation School.

Above: Meteor N.F.14 WS744 seen here has the black and light red fuselage checkerboard markings of No 85 Sqn.

Bottom: Twenty-five Meteor N.F.11s were supplied to the French Air Force and the one seen here at the CEV (Centre d'Essais en Vol, Bretigny), serialled NF11 No 3, was used to flight test an SFECMAS/Nord S.600 ramjet mounted under the starboard wing.

The Meteor F.III

The Meteor F.III was the first version to go into large-scale production, 280 of this mark being built in all, and the first production F.III, EE230, made its maiden flight in September 1944. The first 15 production aircraft (EE230-EE244), with the manufacturer's designation G.41C, had the 1,700-lb (771-kg) s.t. Welland I powerplants. The remaining F.IIIs, designated G.41D, had the RB.37 Derwent I turbojets of 2,000-lb (907-kg) s.t. with better specific fuel consumption as well as provision for a 100-gal (455-litre) ventral fuel tank under the fuselage connected to the main fuselage tank, the capacity of which was slightly greater than the Meteor F.I's. The F.III also differed from the earlier mark in having a rearward-sliding clear-view cockpit canopy instead of a sideways-opening one, and later production aircraft featured a gyro gunsight and had provision for a 180-gal (818-litre) under-fuselage tank. The short engine nacelles of both the Welland- and Derwent-engined variants had caused buffeting to occur at comparatively low Mach numbers, and flight tests with tufting had shown that the airflow broke away where the short, highly curved nacelle met the wing, the resulting buffeting limiting the speed. This was cured by fitting lengthened nacelles to the last 30 Meteor F.IIIs built, this variant being designated G.41E. The longer nacelles greatly improved the streamlining, although at some cost in weight, and they became standard on all subsequent marks.

Below: The Meteor F.III was the first version to go into large-scale production, the first 15 having Welland I engines and the rest, like EE314 seen here, being powered by Derwent Is.

Right: The last 30 Meteor F.IIIs built had lengthened engine nacelles to cure the buffeting caused at comparatively low Mach numbers by the original short engine nacelle shape. These nacelles were made standard for all later marks.

Far right: Meteor F.III EE416 was modified to accommodate a passenger in the ammunition bay behind the pilot to test the prototype Martin-Baker ejector seat. On 24 July 1946 Bernard Lynch made the first live ejection in the UK in the prototype seat from EE416 over Chalgrove in Buckinghamshire.

Below: To test the feasibility of a ground-level ejection Meteor T.7 WA634 was fitted with a modified Martin-Baker Mk 3 seat in the rear cockpit. Using this, Sqn Ldr J. S. Fifield DFC, AFC achieved the first live ejection on the runway in WA634 at Chalgrove on 3 September 1955.

The first unit to equip with Meteor F.IIIs was the pioneer Meteor squadron, No. 616 at Manston, and by the end of January 1945 their Meteor F.Is had been replaced by F.IIIs, the first of this mark having been delivered to the squadron on 18 December 1944. One flight of F.IIIs joined No. 84 Group of the 2nd TAF at Melsbroek airfield near Brussels on 20 January 1945.

On 1 April the squadron moved into the Netherlands, occupying

successively airfields at Gilze-Rijen and Nijmegen, and beginning ground-attack sorties in support of the advancing Allied armies on 16 April. On 20 April the squadron crossed into Germany with a short stay at Quackenbruck and then at Fassberg, before moving on to Luneberg on 3 May, the German surrender being signed on Luneberg Heath five days later. On 7 May the squadron moved on to Lubeck a few miles from the Baltic and remained there until it was disbanded on 29 August 1945.

Rather disappointingly, the Meteor was destined never actually to meet the Me 262 in air-to-air combat, and both No. 616 and the second Meteor F.III unit to form, No. 504 Sqn, used their jets solely on ground-attack sorties in the last weeks of the war in Europe. The latter unit, formed in March 1928 as No. 504 (County of Nottingham) Sqn was flying Spitfire IXs on fighter sweeps and escort missions when it moved to Colerne in March 1945 to re-equip with Meteor F.IIIs. Like No. 616, it also moved to the Continent, returning to Colerne on 10 August 1945, when it was renumbered as No. 245 Squadron. Under its new identity the squadron continued to fly Meteors as part of the air defence of the UK. It operated F.IIIs from August 1945 to March 1948 and Meteor F.IVs from November 1947 to June 1950, when these were replaced by F.8s which were flown until March 1957. No. 616 Sqn, after a post-war spell as a night fighter unit with Mosquito N.F.30s, resumed Meteor F.3 operations as a day fighter unit at Finningley in December 1948, flying this mark until May 1950, F.4s from April 1950 to December 1951, and then F.8s until March 1957.

Fighter Command's first post-war jet fighter wing, based at Bentwaters in Suffolk, was equipped with Meteor F.IIIs of Nos. 56, 74 and 245 Squadrons. No. 56 flew F.IIIs from April 1946 to September 1948. F.4s replaced

them from August 1948 to December 1950 when they were in turn replaced by F.8s, which lasted until February 1954. No. 74 Sqn had completed converting from Spitfire XVIEs to Meteor F.IIIs in June 1945. They flew this mark until March 1948, followed by F.4s from December 1947 to October 1950 and then F.8s until March 1957, when Hunters took over. Not long after the first Meteor wing was formed, a second wing was also equipped with F.IIIs and started operations at Boxted, near Colchester. This consisted of Nos. 222, 234 and 263 Squadrons, the first of these flying F.IIIs from October 1945 to June 1947, while No. 263 operated them from the end of August 1945 to March 1948, both these units subsequently flying Meteor F.4s and F.8s. No. 234 Sqn replaced its Spitfire IXs with Meteor F.IIIs in February 1946, but on 1 September that year it was renumbered as No. 266 Sqn and continued to fly its F.IIIs until April 1948. By then they had been replaced by Meteor F.4s, which equipped the unit when it was again renumbered as No. 43 Sqn on 11 February 1949. It continued flying the F.4s under its new identity until September 1950 when Meteor F.8s took over, these being replaced by Hunters from August 1954.

In addition to the first two jet fighter wings, and Nos. 504 and 616 Squadrons, Meteor F.IIIs equipped five other fighter squadrons. Also, the Auxiliary Air Force, which had been reformed on 10 May 1946, received its first Meteors on 14 August 1948 when F.3s began to equip No. 500 (County of Kent) Sqn at West Malling. These were flown until October 1951 and were followed by F.4s, operated from July 1951 to February 1952 and by F.8s, which the squadron was flying when the Royal Auxiliary Air Force was disbanded on 10 March 1957.

Several Meteor F.IIIs were used for various test or experimental purposes, such as EE479 and

EE416 used for Martin-Baker ejector seat trials, as described in the next chapter. F.III EE240/G went to the United States for evaluation and another F.III became NZ6001 of the Royal New Zealand Air Force. F.III EE397 was used for some early flight refuelling trials and EE360/G, the first to be fitted with the lengthened engine nacelles, became in effect the prototype Meteor F.IV.

From April to June 1948, deck landing trials were done by two Meteor F.IIIs – EE337 and EE387 – which culminated in a series of 32 carrier landings on HMS *Implacable* by two A.&A.E.E. pilots from Boscombe Down between 10-18 June. For these trials both Meteors had the Derwent 5 engines of the F.IV fitted in the short nacelles, an undercarriage strengthened to absorb a deck landing velocity of 11.5 ft/second (3.5 m/s), and a Sea Hornet-type V-frame arrestor hook fitted under the strengthened rear fuselage about 12 ft (3.6 m) aft of the wing trailing edge. All non-essential equipment was deleted to lighten the aircraft, and the inner wheel doors were removed to avoid the risk of damage from the carrier's arrestor wires; this made it necessary to limit the maximum speed to 346 mph (557 km/h). Although designed with no thought of carrier operations in mind, the Meteor was found in these trials to be an excellent deck-landing aircraft with especially good take-off characteristics, and it was felt to have better handling qualities than any other jet tested at the A.&A.E.E. until then. The view for deck landing was excellent, and power-on approaches were made at a steady rate of descent at 85-90 knots IAS. However, this high praise did not lead to a production order for the Meteor as a carrier-based fighter as the Royal Navy was already committed to the Supermarine Attacker, but Meteor F.4 EE531 was later used for wing-folding tests.

Ejector seat trials

The Meteor played an important part in the development of an outstanding British contribution to aviation safety, the Martin-Baker range of ejector seats. Escaping from combat aircraft was a problem that had become increasingly difficult as fighter speeds had risen, and with jet fighters going into production it had now become a critical consideration. After a meeting held at the RAE in January 1944 to consider the problem, an approach was made for a possible solution to Mr James Martin, chief designer and managing director of Martin-Baker Aircraft Co Ltd. The firm had designed and produced several successful emergency devices, as well as a series of fighter prototypes, culminating in the brilliant M.B.5. Martin-Baker had produced 250,000 cartridge-operated barrage balloon cable cutters for fitting in the wing leading edges of Bomber Command aircraft, and also a jettisonable cockpit hood for the Spitfire that was fitted in time for the Battle of Britain.

In 1944 an ejector seat was not considered a practical proposition because of the space and obstacle-clearance limitations of current fighter cockpits. The first idea for an ejection device took the form of a swinging arm on top of the fuselage, hinged at the rear and with hooks on the front end to engage in rings on the pilot's parachute harness to pluck him out of the cockpit; initial movement of the arm was by springs, with an aerodynamic follow-through. This concept was discarded in favour of an ejectable seat propelled up a guide rail and out of the aircraft by means of an explosive charge in an ejection gun, which comprised two

telescoping tubes. Static firings of the seat began on an 18-ft (5.5-m) inclined plane test rig, on which Mr Bernard Lynch, an experimental fitter with Martin-Baker, made the first live test on 24 January 1945. Information was gradually built up on the human g-tolerances, especially that of the spine, to ejection accelerations, and various modifications were made to the seat design. The seat was installed in Boulton Paul Defiant DR344, loaned from the MAP, and on 11 May 1945 this made the first in-flight ejection in the UK with a dummy load, when flown at Wittering by Brian Greenstead, the chief test pilot of Rotol. On 17 May, six more dummy ejections were made at Beaulieu up to a speed of 300 mph (483 km/h).

Seat development continued on a new 65-ft (20-m) test rig at Martin-Baker's Denham airfield, which allowed for higher ejection velocities. An important addition, which was made following tests on this rig, was the introduction of a face blind to prevent the head being thrown forward during ejection. This also served to protect the face from slipstream, as well as providing a means of firing the seat cartridge and preventing sideways movement of the head. On 12 September 1945 Martin-Baker received an MAP contract for the design, development and manufacture of two 'pilot ejection units', and Meteor F.III EE416 was delivered to Denham on 6 November that year for these seats to be installed, one for the pilot and one for the passenger seated directly behind him in the ammunition bay. Various structural modification and local strengthening were necessary to cater for the ejection loads. With these completed, the Meteor went to Chalgrove aerodrome, Oxfordshire, where static tests began on 8 June 1946 into a specially erected net at the top of a 45-ft (14-m) tower. On 24 June the first dummy flight ejection was made from the

Meteor at 415 mph (668 km/h), but the main parachute used to retrieve the seat opened too early and consequently burst. This happened a second time, and it was realised that the small drogue deployed immediately after ejection to stabilise and decelerate the seat was being drawn into the wake of the seat and becoming entangled. This snag was eventually cured by devising a drogue 'gun' on the side of the seat which was tripped as it left the aircraft, thus deploying the drogue via a nylon cord.

On 24 July 1946 the first live ejection from the prototype seat was made by Bernard Lynch from Meteor F.III EE416, piloted by Capt J.E.D. Scott, and flying at 8,000 ft (2,438 m) and 320 mph (515 km/h) over Chalgrove. This was the UK's first live ejection, although not the first in the world – Herr Buss, the chief test parachutist at Rechlin, the German equivalent of Farnborough, had made three test ejections during the war, and the Heinkel He 280 twin-jet fighter had the first ejection seat ever to be developed, operated by compressed air. The US Navy was the first of many export customers for Martin-Baker, having early on ordered a 110-ft (33.5-m) test rig and an ejection seat. After this was installed in the rear cockpit of a Douglas JD-1 Invader, Lt Furtek, USN, made a successful live ejection on 1 November 1946, this being the first in the Western hemisphere. In February that year a second Meteor F.III EE479, had been delivered to Denham for installation of a production ejector seat, and further live tests were postponed while the prototype seat was being redesigned on a production basis. In June 1947 the Ministry of Supply, which had succeeded the MAP, decided to standardise the Martin-Baker ejector seat, known as the Mk 1 in production form, for all new RAF aircraft. The Mk 1 seat began dummy air tests immediately and, after 35 such tests plus three more live tests, the design of the drogue and its stowage was finally perfected.

Bernard Lynch made his second ejection, once again entirely successfully, on 11 August 1947 from 6,000 ft (1,829 m), and on 29 August he made another successful ejection from the Meteor at a TAS of 505 mph (813 km/h) at 12,000 ft (3,658 m); despite the slipstream blast at this speed he suffered no ill effects. Lynch made a number of other ejections, including one at 30,000 ft (9,144 m) and in 1948 was awarded the British Empire Medal in recognition of his personal courage and pioneering work in live test ejections. A French Air Force pilot, Lt Cartier, made three ejections with the Mk 1 seat in EE479, the second of which, at Bretigny on 9 June 1948, was the fastest ever made up to that time, at 515 mph (829 km/h) TAS at 6,000 ft (1,829 m). More than 15 live descents and many dummy tests went to prove the Mk 1 seat's reliability before it went into production and, as the Mk 1E, it was installed as standard in the Meteor F.8. Other types with the same basic seat were the Attacker, Wyvern naval strike aircraft, Canberra, Sea Hawk and Venom.

Meteor F.4 VT150 was used for the trial installation of the Martin-Baker Mk 1E seat. This necessitated moving the windscreen forward, fitting a completely new one-piece cockpit hood, cutting out the centre of the seat bulkhead and sloping it back to achieve the optimum 25° recline for the seat back, fitting a retractable gyro gunsight and making a number of smaller modifications to instruments and controls. VT150 was later fitted with the Meteor F.8's tail unit and the 30-in (76-cm) forward fuselage extension of the F.8 to become the second prototype of that mark.

The first successful emergency ejection with a Mk 1 seat had been made on 20 March 1951 from an Attacker by a Royal Navy pilot after engine failure, and within five years of this Martin-Baker seats had been supplied to 24 countries. With the Mk 1, the pilot separated himself manually from the seat during his descent, but as early as 1947 it was clear that the manual method would not be suitable at high altitudes. Martin-Baker, aided by both US Navy and USAF orders for automatic equipment, began working towards the fully automatic seat, which entered production as the Mk 2 for the Hunter, Swift and Gloster Javelin. The Mk 2 seat's automatic operation was achieved by a Martin-Baker patent time release mechanism with a barostat control which unfastened the seat harness to free the occupant and at the same time uncoupled the drogue, which opened the pilot's parachute by an extension line. At high altitudes, the barostat control provided for the pilot to fall in the seat, with an automatically turned-on oxygen supply, until 10,000 ft (3,048 m) was passed, his seat harness being released five seconds after this. The pilot was then tipped out of his seat through the action of the drogue, and the seat fell away. From the start of Mk 2 seat development, it had been intended to convert the Mk 1 seats already fitted to automatic operation, and the Meteor F.8 and other types fitted with these seats had them converted to Mk 2 standard with the addition of the time release mechanism, the F.8's seat now being known as the Mk 2E.

Having made the seat safe for use at high altitudes, attention was now turned to lowering the minimum height of 400 ft (122 m) at which the Mk 2 seat could safely be used. This was done by developing a Duplex drogue system of two drogues in tandem to deploy the pilot's main parachute, enabling the delay of five seconds after ejection necessary before the single drogue could be deployed to be reduced to three. When fitted to the Mk 3 seat with a higher ejection velocity of 80 ft/second (24 m/sec), developed for the V-bombers to clear their tall fins, this made a safe ejection possible down to 50 ft (15 m). It now became possible to explore the feasibility of a genuine zero-feet ejection with the aircraft still on the ground, and Meteor T.7/8 WA634 was modified to incorporate a Mk 3 seat in the rear with a Duplex drogue system and the automatic time release modified to give only 1½ seconds delay. Extensive tests with dummies confirmed that with ejection in this seat from WA634 shortly before take-off, separation and full deployment of the pilot's parachute took place with about 20-30 ft (6-9 m) to spare.

The first live ejection from the runway was made by Sqn Ldr J.S. Fifield DFC, AFC, in the Meteor at Chalgrove on 3 September 1955; he used a 24 ft (7 m) diameter Irving Mk 9 back-type parachute and the entire sequence, from ejection to his safe touch-down, occupied only about six seconds. On 25 October that year Sqn Ldr Fifield followed this remarkable achievement by an ejection at over 40,000 ft (12,192 m) and 242 mph (389 km/h) in the same Meteor over Chalgrove, which was accompanied by Meteor F.R.9 VZ438 from the RAE Farnborough as a chase 'plane to photograph the ejection. Sqn Ldr Fifield landed safely after falling for nearly three minutes in the seat, stabilised by the Duplex drogue, before separating from it automatically just below 10,000 ft (3,048 m). For his services to ejector seat development, he was awarded a Queen's Commendation for Valuable Services in the Air in the 1956 New Year's Honours List.

The advantages of the Duplex drogue system in reducing the minimum ejection height were considered sufficiently great to justify an extensive retrofit programme to fit all seats except those in the Canberra – about 6,000 seats in all – with the new Duplex drogue system.

Breaking the world speed record

The G.41F Meteor F.IV differed from the F.III chiefly in having the more powerful Derwent V turbojets of 3,500 lb (1,587 kg) s.t., this mark of Derwent being basically a scaled-down version of the larger Rolls-Royce Nene to fit the Meteor airframe. This gave the F.IV about twice the total thrust of the F.9/40 prototypes and the Meteor F.I, and led to a much-improved performance and better handling qualities; the F.IV could do over 400 mph (644 km/h) at sea level flying on one engine! This mark also had the longer engine nacelles featured on the last 30 Meteor F.IIIs, and a very early modification introduced on the F.IV was a reduction of 5 ft 10 in (1.8 m) in wing span to 37 ft 2 in (11.3 m) to improve the rate of roll and the speed, and also the stress factors in the centre-section spars. The clipped wings were first fitted early in 1946 to EE455, one of the two Meteors used in the first post-war attempt on the World Air Speed Record. Some early production F.IVs were in fact retrospectively modified to have the clipped wings before delivery to the RAF.

The Meteor F.IV prototype, EE360/G, was modified from an F.III and made its first flight as an F.IV in July 1945; the production F.IVs later conformed to Specification F.11/46. It was decided to make the first jet attempt on the World Absolute Air Speed Record with the Meteor F.IV to show the sort of speeds of which jet propulsion was now capable. The existing record of 468.94 mph (755.138 km/h) had been set up on 26 April 1939 by Fritz Wendel in the Messerschmitt

Me 209V1 prototype which the Germans, for propaganda purposes and to deceive foreign air forces, had represented as the 'Bf 109R', a specially modified version of the well-known Bf 109. During the war piston-engined fighter speeds in combat had got ever closer to this figure, which was well within the reach of jets. Two Meteor F.IIIs, EE454 and EE455, were accordingly fitted with prototype Derwent 5 engines for the first post-war attempt on the record, so becoming in effect F.IV prototypes, and they differed hardly at all from standard production F.IVs. All apertures such as the cannon ports were sealed off, the radio mast and guns were removed and a highly polished surface finish was applied; EE454, to be named 'Britannia', retained its standard Service camouflage and markings, and was flown by Group Capt H. J. Wilson, AFC, while EE455, flown by Mr Eric Greenwood, who had succeeded Michael Daunt as Gloster's chief test pilot in June 1944, was painted yellow all over and known as the 'Yellow Peril'.

A 3-km (1.86-miles) Speed Course was laid out at Herne Bay, off the north Kent coast near Whitstable, with two 6½-km (4-miles) anti-clockwise turns at 500 mph (804.6 km/h) over the Isle of Sheppey and Thanet prior to the runs in each direction over the

Speed Course. The complete circuit was approximately 33 miles (53 km) long, the Meteors taking off and landing at Manston for each flight. Under the 'Code Sportif' regulations of the FAI (Federation Aéronautique Internationale), dating back to the pioneering days of flying, the record runs had to be flown at a mere 246 ft (75 m) altitude, which called for considerable skill from the pilots at the speeds the Meteors would attain. Group Capt Wilson, then Commanding Officer of the Empire Test Pilots School at Boscombe Down, who was in charge of the course and responsible for its layout, had previously been chief test pilot at the RAE, Farnborough, and had flown the Gloster E.28/39 and some of the F.9/40 prototypes. But, even with his and Greenwood's experience of high speed flight, it was still thought prudent to provide a line of 30 'K'-type yellow dinghies parallel to the Speed Course, as well as a patrolling Supermarine Walrus and high-speed air-sea rescue launches. But the risks of flying so low at high speed were offset by the advantage that the air temperature would be highest near to the

EE455, flown in the first post-war speed record attempt by Gloster test pilot Eric Greenwood, was yellow all over and unofficially known as the 'Yellow Peril'. It is seen here mounted on jacks for display.

ground, and sound travelled at its fastest, so that the highest Mach number could be attained.

After waiting nearly seven weeks for the best possible atmospheric conditions, the record attempt was made on 7 November 1945. Group Capt Wilson, flying EE454 'Britannia', broke the record with an average speed of 606 mph (975 km/h) from four runs over the course, two in each direction; his fastest run was at 610 mph (981.6 km/h) and his slowest at 592 mph (952.7 km/h). Eric Greenwood, in the yellow EE455, averaged 603 mph for his four runs. A second attempt for still higher speeds might well have been made shortly after, but it was found that some rivets in the fairing over the main spar of EE454, near one of the intakes, had pulled out after Group Capt Wilson's fastest run (his last one), and it was decided to postpone any second attempt until a full examination had been made of both aircraft; there was no other damage, although a fair amount of paint was stripped from both Meteors during the record runs. Skin friction at high speed raised the temperature in the cockpit by about 30°F, and Eric Greenwood admitted to perspiring rather freely as a result.

For the second post-war attempt on the Speed Record, the RAF High Speed Flight was reformed at Tangmere, Sussex, on 14 June 1946 and a course similar to the one at Herne Bay was laid out just off the coast, with turning points off Littlehampton and near West Worthing. Leader of the Flight was Group Capt E.M. Donaldson, DSO, AFC, and the two other pilots were Flt Lt Neville Duke, DSO, OBE, DFC, and Gloster test pilot Sqn Ldr W.A. 'Bill' Waterton, AFC. Three standard Meteor F.IVs, EE528, EE529 and EE530, were used for practice runs, and to holidaymakers and residents alike they became a familiar sight that summer on their low-level runs past beaches that still carried the

coastal defence barriers of triangular tubular frames put up to stop the German tanks coming ashore in 1940.

Two specially-modified Meteor F.IVs, EE549 and EE550, were used for the record attempt itself; these had the cannon removed and the gun ports faired over, the air brakes locked down and a highly polished finish with all cracks, dents and minor surface irregularities filled in or removed. A 43-gal (195-litre) fuel tank was installed in the magazine bay with two extra tanks of 13 gals (59 litres) each, one in each gun bay. Even so, an extra 563 lb (255 kg) of ballast was necessary to compensate for the deleted cannon, and this gave an all-up weight of 14,075 lb (6,384 kg) in record-breaking trim. The standard cockpit canopies fitted suffered at first from softening and distortion as a result of the temperature rise caused by skin friction at high speeds – a factor that had been present in the previous record attempt – and so the perspex canopies were replaced by special metal ones with small transparent windows on the F.IVs used for practice as well as on EE549 and EE550. Before the record attempt on 7 September, both of these were fitted with Derwent 5s with a special 'sprint' rating of 4,200 lb (1,905 kg) s.t.

On 7 September the weather was not too good, with low cloud, steady drizzle and a low air temperature, as well as a SSW wind gusting at 5-12 mph (8-19 km/h), but Group Capt Donaldson took off first in EE549 at 5.45 pm; he landed 14 minutes later after having broken the record with an average speed of 616 mph (991 km/h) on four runs. Sqn Ldr Waterton, taking off not long after in EE550, averaged 614 mph (988 km/h) on his four runs. Because the weather had been so poor, a second attempt on the record over the same course was made on 24 September, in which 29 flights were made altogether.

Although the speed of 1,000 km/h (621.26 mph) was exceeded on one of these runs, the average did not go above 616 mph. Three attempts were made by Donaldson, and one each by Bill Waterton and Neville Duke. A nasty moment occurred during Donaldson's second attempt when the rudder mass balance broke off, causing violent vibration and a momentary loss of control but Donaldson recovered and completed all four runs. Later the rudder on EE549 was changed and he made a third attempt. Duke was disqualified on his third run for having dived as he entered the course.

Since this second attempt was not successful in raising the record speed, the Air Ministry gave permission for both the Supermarine E.10/44 Attacker prototype and the swept-wing de Havilland D.H.108 to attempt the record over the same course. However, on 27 September the D.H.108 prototype broke up over the Thames Estuary in a high speed run when travelling at, or close to, Mach 1. Geoffrey de Havilland Jr, the pilot, was killed and this put paid to any further record attempts for the time being. The record-breaking EE549 was displayed at the first post-war Paris Salon de l'Aeronautique held in the Grand Palais from 15 November to 1 December 1946 together with a standard F.IV EE590, and on its return flight, flown by Sqn Ldr W. A. Waterton, it set up a new Paris-London record of 520 mph (837 km/h). On 19 January 1947, Waterton broke this record again in EE549 when he flew between turning points at Paris le Bourget and Croydon Airport in a mere 20 minutes 11 seconds, averaging 618.4 mph (995 km/h) between the two cities. It was later used as a personal 'hack' by Air Chief Marshal Sir James Robb until 1948, finished blue overall with Sir James's initials 'JMR' in white. EE549 later became a 'gate guardian' at RAF Innsworth, Gloucestershire, only

Meteor F.IVs EE549 and EE550 were specially modified for the second post-war speed record attempt in the summer of 1946. EE549 flown by Group Capt E. M. Donaldson DSO, AFC broke the record on 7 September, and is seen here in its present home in the RAF Museum at Hendon. The original cockpit canopy was replaced by a special metal-framed one to withstand high speed skin friction better.

about four miles from where it was built, and it is now displayed in the RAF Museum at Hendon.

Several other records were also set up by Meteors. On 6 February

1948, a standard F.IV VT103, flown by Bill Waterton, raised the World 100 km closed-circuit speed record to 542.9 mph (873.6 km/h) flying on a triangular course from Moreton Valence. This record was broken by John Derry in a D.H. 108 on 12 April that year but, on 12 May 1950, James Cooksey in a Meteor F.8 set a record for speed over a distance of 1,000 km of 510.92 mph (822.22 km/h). Several point-to-point speed records between cities were also set up in Meteors; Gloster's F.IV G-AIDC, while being flown on a demonstration tour of Europe by Sqn Ldr D.V. Cotes-

Preedy on 22 April 1947, set a Brussels-Copenhagen speed record of 630 mph (1,013.8 km/h). On 4 April 1950, Gloster's acting chief test pilot, Sqn Ldr Jan Zurakowski, set up a London-Copenhagen-London record time of 2 hours, 29 minutes, 8 seconds, in Meteor F.8 VZ468 giving a speed of 480.29 mph (770.202 km/h) for the out-and-return journey between the two capitals. The Copenhagen-London leg of this flight was also confirmed as a record, taking 1 hour, 11 minutes, 17 seconds, at a speed of 500.37 mph (805.752 km/h).

The Meteor F.IV

The production Meteor F.IV was the first mark truly to show the basic airframe's potentialities, as the more powerful Derwent V turbojets gave a much-improved performance and completely invalidated the earlier criticisms of poor take-off and initial rate of climb that had been made of the lower-powered F.9/40 prototypes and Meteor F.Is. The F.IV had so much power that it was now easy to exceed the limiting Mach number of 0.8 even in level flight, but a good safety feature was that it would pitch up gently when the edge of compressibility was reached. The tendency to 'snake' was less on the F.IV than it had been in earlier versions, and to lose height quickly the use of air brakes was essential; these gave a swift deceleration, up to 0.8G at 400 mph (644 km/h). The clipped wings reducing the span to 37 ft 2 in (11.3 m) were introduced following the loss of a Meteor flown by Gloster test pilot Moss,

which broke up in the air after a very rapid pull-out from an apparently misjudged dive, and this reduced span became standard on most later marks. The F.IV was also the first mark to have a fully operational pressure cabin, which gave a cabin pressure differential of 3 lb/sq in at 24,000 ft (7,315 m) and which was the only one of its time to operate on air bled directly from the engine compressor casings. A TR. 1143 two-way vhf radio (later a TR. 1464 vhf set) was installed with provision for beam approach, and radar identification was provided by an R.3121 IFF (Identification Friend or Foe) installation. Later production F.IVs could be fitted with underwing drop tanks for ferry flights only and, for ferry or operational flights, a 180 gal (818 litres) ventral tank could be carried.

Altogether, 657 Meteor F.IVs were built, 465 of them for the RAF, of which the last 45 (serialled VZ386-VZ429 plus VZ436) were constructed at Coventry by Sir W.G. Armstrong Whitworth Aircraft Ltd, the Hawker Siddeley Group associate company of Gloster, who were entrusted with the development of the Meteor night fighters. Seven of the 45, to have been numbered VZ420-

VZ426, went to the Egyptian Air Force. VZ436 was the last F.IV to be built and was delivered in April 1950 from Baginton; the first Armstrong Whitworth-built F.IV had flown in 1949.

With camouflage superseded by the post-war all-silver colour scheme, all F.IVs were finished in a silver dope polished to a high gloss. The first squadron to re-equip with Meteor F.IVs was No. 222 in June 1947, followed by Nos. 245 and 263 in November that year and No. 74 in December 1947. Many squadrons operated Meteor F.IIIs, F.IVs and F.8s in succession, flying their 'Meatboxes' (as pilots affectionately called the aircraft) until replaced, usually by Hunters or until the squadron disbanded. In addition to Nos. 500 (County of Kent), 504 (County of Nottingham) and 616 Squadrons, which flew F.IVs after earlier operating F.IIIs, four other Auxiliary Air Force units equipped with F.IVs. These were No. 600 (City of London) Sqn at Biggin Hill, No. 610 (County of Chester) Sqn at Hooton Park, No. 611 (West Lancashire) Sqn at Woodvale and No. 615 (County of Surrey) Sqn, also at Biggin Hill. These F.IVs served the Auxiliary squadrons for only a short time – usually about a year or so – before being replaced by Meteor F.8s, which were flown until the Royal Auxiliary Air Force was disbanded on 10 March 1957. Some F.IVs continued to serve in training units such as the Advanced Flying Schools after being replaced by F.8s in first-line squadrons.

On 7 and 8 July 1950, a Royal Air Force Flying Display was staged at Farnborough that recalled, in size and scope, those memorable RAF Displays of pre-war days at Hendon. Meteors played a prominent part in this event, and the items included formation aerobatics by four F.4s of No. 263 Sqn, and the defence of the airfield

In 1949 the Belgian Air Force ordered 48 Meteor F.4s, the last of which, serialled EF48, is seen here. They equipped Nos 349, 350 and four Squadrons of the 1st Fighter Wing.

from a mock attack by 12 Mosquito N.F.36s and seven Hornet F.R.3s by 15 Meteor F.4s of Nos. 66 and 92 Squadrons, plus a T.7 of No. 92 Sqn. After being 'scrambled', the Meteors formed up and intercepted the attackers, which were driven off; the Meteors then made a stream landing and were refuelled and rearmed. Later, in the culminating fly-past of the display, there were 24 Meteors, mostly F.4s except for one or two T.7s, from six Fighter Command squadrons in formation, and 12 Belgian Air Force Meteor F.4s in the contingent representing NATO and the Commonwealth countries. At the Royal Air Force Coronation Review at Odiham, Hampshire, on 15 July 1953 many Meteors of different marks were displayed both on the ground and in the air, and the fly-past included nine formations of 24 Meteor F.8s each from nine different Fighter Command stations flying over in succession – surely the largest number of the type ever seen in the air at one time.

The Meteor had obvious export possibilities for sale to countries equipping with jet fighters for the first time, and Gloster built an F.IV demonstrator for their own use on overseas sales tours. Registered G-AIDC, this was the first jet aircraft on the British civil register, and was painted an attractive scarlet all over, with cream registration letters and fuselage flash; its Certificate of Airworthiness was issued on 14 April 1947. In May 1947, when it was being flown by a Belgian pilot at Melsbroek, one undercarriage leg extended at 550 mph (885 km/h), and G-AIDC went into a series of violent upward rolls. The pilot succeeded in regaining control but the aircraft was damaged beyond repair when the weakened undercarriage leg collapsed on landing. In spite of

Royal Netherlands Air Force Meteor F.4 1.69 (ex-VZ407) is seen here in the Dutch Air Force Museum at Soesterberg. 65 of this mark were supplied to Holland.

this, 48 Meteor F.4s were ordered for the Belgian Air Force in 1949 and deliveries of these, plus the first two Meteor T.7s for Belgium, began in June that year. They were serialled EF 1 to EF 48 and equipped Nos. 349, 350 and 4 Squadrons of the 1st Fighter Wing; they were later supplemented by a further batch of ex-RAF F.4s. From 1951 they began to be replaced by Meteor F.8s and were transferred to the Operational Training Unit at Coxyde; some were later converted to T.7s by Avions Fairey SA at Gosselies, and the F.4s finally became obsolete in 1957.

The first export order for Meteors had been one for 100 F.IVs placed in May 1947 by the Argentine Government for the Fuerza Aerea Argentina. These were shipped out and reassembled in Argentina by Gloster personnel, the last being delivered in September 1948; the first 50 were to have been for the RAF, but the rest were built to Argentine order. They were serialled 1.001 to 1.100, the serials being carried aft of the light blue, white and light blue fuselage roundels and on the tip of the nose. Initially the Meteors equipped one of the two Air Regiments (Fighter), there later being one Fighter and two

Interceptor-Fighter Regiments in the FAA. During the revolution of 1955 that led to the overthrow of General Juan Peron and his subsequent exile in Spain, the FAA Meteors were used by both Government and rebel forces, and at least two were lost in action. In 1960 28 F-86F Sabres were acquired from the USA to succeed the Meteors as first-line fighters, and by 1966 the 28 surviving F.4s were equipping Fighter-Bomber Groups II and III of Air Brigade No. VII, with headquarters at Moron air force base, Buenos Aires, one of the five FAA Air Brigades. They were then beginning to be replaced by the first of 50 ex-US Navy McDonnell-Douglas A-4B Skyhawk attack bombers.

The second export order after Argentina's was placed in June 1947 when the first five of a total of 65 were ordered for the Royal Netherlands Air Force. These were serialled 1.21 to 1.81 and equipped Nos. 322, 323, 326 and 327 Squadrons, later being replaced by Fokker-built Meteor F.8s; the last ones were phased out in 1962. In 1949 Denmark ordered 20 Meteor F.4s for the Royal Danish Naval Air Service, and deliveries of these, which were serialled D.461 to D.480, began in October that year,

all of them going to equip *3 Luftflotille* at Karup. On 1 October 1950 the Naval Air Service merged with the Army Air Corps to form the Royal Danish Air Force, and the F.4s, plus five Meteor T.7s, were the most modern type in the new air arm which, apart from 35 Spitfires, was made up almost entirely of trainers and light transports. The Meteor F.4s now equipped No. 723 Sqn, or *Eskadrille* 723 and, supplemented with 20 Meteor F.8s acquired in 1951 to equip *Eskadrille* 724, formed the nucleus for a considerable expansion of Danish air power and its contribution to NATO in the 1950s and 1960s. The F.4s began to be replaced in *Eskadrille* 723 in November 1952 by the first of 20 Meteor N.F.11s for all-weather interception, and the F.8s of *Eskadrille* 724 were replaced by Hunter F.51s from 1956.

Deliveries of 12 Meteor F.4s to the Egyptian Air Force, serialled 1401 to 1412, began in October 1949 after Egypt had placed an order following the lifting of the arms embargo imposed when the first Arab-Israeli war broke out on the formation of the state of Israel in May 1948. The F.4s were still in service in the mid-1950s and were supplemented by six Meteor T.7s. Meteor F.4 EE523 was sold to France for development work and acquired the 'experimental'

registration F-WEPQ before delivery. It later became F-BEPQ and was used by ONERA (Office Nationale d'Etudes et de Recherches Aéronautiques), the French Government research organisation.

Several other Meteor F.4s were used for various trial or experimental purposes such as EE519, which did flight tests fitted with two 1,000-lb (453-kg) bombs and also with eight 98-lb (44-kg) rocket projectiles. Two F.4s, RA438 and VZ389, were used for air-to-air refuelling trials by Flight Refuelling Ltd, each being fitted with a nose probe connected to the main fuel tank. The first transfer of a fuel load was made on 2 April 1950. To reduce the amount of ballast that the Meteor F.IV had to carry to correct an inherent tail heaviness, F.IV RA382 was fitted with the 30-in (76-cm) forward fuselage extension inserted at the front spar bulkhead joint that became a standard feature of the Meteor F.8; the extra length was used for additional fuel tankage. In this form the F.IV RA382 was sometimes referred to in the contemporary aviation press as the Meteor F.VI, but this projected mark was not in fact built; it was similar in outline to the Meteor F.8. The fuselage extension proved to be a success, although some troubles occurred through the larger shift in the centre of gravity

when using ammunition, the guns now being further forward, and these were not finally cured until the Meteor F.8 tail unit was fitted to RA382, which thus became a prototype F.8.

The first attempt to adapt the Meteor for photo reconnaissance was when F.IV VT347 was fitted with a camera installation to become the sole Meteor P.R.V. Two F.36 vertical cameras were fitted in the rear fuselage, and an oblique F.24 camera on a mounting in the nose, which had three optically flat windows as camera ports. The F.24 could be set on the ground to shoot straight ahead or obliquely to port or starboard, and the normal armament was still carried. On its first flight on 13 July 1949, the P.R.V prototype broke up in the air during a very fast run over Gloster's Moreton Valence aerodrome, killing the pilot, Rodney Dryland. The P.R.V did not go into production, but a very similar camera installation was featured in the later Meteor P.R.10.

Three of the 12 Meteor F.4s delivered to the Egyptian Air Force from October 1949 seen over the Pyramids. Armstrong Whitworth built seven of the Egyptian F.4s.

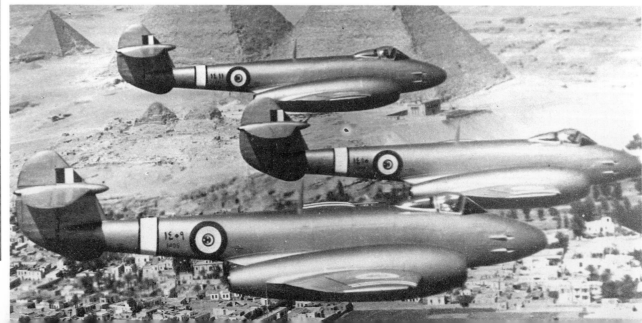

The Meteor Trainer

As the gap in speed between advanced piston-engined trainers such as the Harvard and Boulton Paul Balliol, and high speed jet fighters such as the Meteor F.4, was already quite considerable, and would obviously widen as fighter speeds grew closer to and passed the supersonic, a two-seater advanced trainer version of the Meteor was a logical step. This emerged as the Meteor T.7 which had the 30 in (76 cm) extension of the forward fuselage to take a second seat and dual controls under a continuous cockpit canopy that hinged sideways to starboard for opening. Armament was deleted and no military load was carried, but there was provision for two 100-gal (454-litres) underwing drop tanks, as well as the 180-gal

Prototype G-43 Meteor T.7, registered as G-AKPK, in the red and cream finish which it wore during its demonstration flight to Paris in 1948.

(818-litres) under-fuselage tank. Apart from these changes, the airframe and Derwent 5 engines were the same as the F.4's. There was provision for a camera gun and gyro gunsight, and amber screens could be fitted in the cockpit for instrument training.

The prototype G.43 Meteor T.7, registered G-AKPK, was built by Gloster as a private venture, and used the wings, rear fuselage and tail unit of the F.4 demonstrator G-AIDC which had been badly damaged in the accident at Melsbroek in May 1947. G-AKPK made its first flight on 19 March 1948 and left on its first overseas sales tour, of Turkey, in May 1948; like the earlier civil Meteor, it was finished in an attractive red all over, with cream registration letters, fuselage flash and lettering on the forward fuselage. On 30 September 1948 it flew a letter from the Lord Mayor of London, Sir Frederick M. Wells, to M. Pierre de Gaulle, President of the Municipal Council of Paris, as part of Operation 'Hare and Tortoise', sponsored by *The Aeroplane* to carry a letter from the centre of London to that of Paris in under an hour, demonstrating the improvement in city centre-to-city centre times theoretically made possible by a combination of helicopters and jets.

Taking off from the National Car Park at the east end of St Paul's Cathedral in Bristol Type 171 Sycamore prototype VL958, Mr E. A. Swiss flew to Biggin Hill in nine minutes, 35 seconds, with the letter, which was quickly handed over to Sqn Ldr W. A. Waterton and Eric Greenwood in the Meteor T.7 G-AKPK who, with engines running, were away in 49 seconds. In spite of overshooting Paris Orly in poor visibility and a very low cloud base, they landed there only 27 minutes, 38 seconds later, having averaged 465 mph (748 km/h) over the 214 miles (344 km) from Biggin Hill. The letter was then flown by Alan Bristow in Westland-Sikorsky S.51 G-AJHW to the Place des Invalides in Paris, where it was handed over. The total elapsed time from St Paul's to the Invalides was 46 minutes, 44.8 seconds, Mr Bristow having flown the last leg in the S.51 in 8½ minutes. This compared to just over an hour for BEA's normal airline flights with Vickers Vikings from London Northolt to Paris le Bourget, plus another 2¾ hours needed for transport to and from these airfields to the airline terminals, and for formalities. The Meteor T.7 G-AKPK was sold to the Royal Netherlands Air Force in November 1948, acquiring the Dutch serial I-1. A second prototype T.7 was converted from

F.4 EE530 in 1948, and some years later was fitted with an F.8 tail unit and the camera nose section of a Meteor F.R.9. Another T.7, WL375, also had the F.R.9 nose and F.8 tail unit, and was used as a camera ship by the RAE at Farnborough. Meteor T.7 VW411, which later had an F.8 tail unit, was also fitted with the camera nose of the P.R.10, and another T.7 with this same nose was VZ649.

A production order for the Meteor T.7 had by then been placed for the RAF, covered by Air Ministry Specification T.1/47, and the first production T.7, VW410, made its maiden flight on 26 October 1948. In December that year the T.7 became the first jet trainer to go into RAF service, and the new mark was employed at Advanced Flying Schools to convert to jets pilots who had already obtained their wings on Harvards or Balliol T.2s. The first of these Meteor T.7 conversion courses, which lasted for 14 or 18 weeks each, started at No. 203 Advanced Flying School (formerly No. 226 Operational Conversion Unit) at Driffield, Yorkshire, in the spring of 1949. By this time Fighter Command was almost completely re-equipped with jets such as Meteor F.4s and Vampire F.B.5s, although Mosquito N.F.36s still equipped the night fighter squadrons and some Auxiliary Air Force units were flying Spitfires. When the Jet Provost/Vampire T.11 jet training sequence was introduced in 1954, the need for the Advanced Flying Schools was removed and the Meteor T.7s were no longer first-line jet trainers. They continued to be used at both RAF and Royal Auxiliary Air Force stations for refresher flying and continuation training and also as station 'hacks'. A number of T.7s were also supplied to the Royal Navy. Later production T.7s had the uprated Derwent 8 engines of 3,600 lb (1,633 kg) s.t. as fitted to the Meteor F.8, and some T.7s had the F.8 tail unit as well. The last Meteor T.7 to be built was XF279,

which was delivered in July 1954, and rather surprisingly more T.7s were built – a total of 712 – than F.4s.

The T.7 found a ready sale to those countries that had ordered Meteor F.4s or were buying F.8s. The Belgian Air Force acquired some T.7s to convert pilots to its Meteor F.4s, the first two being delivered in June 1949, and some F.4s were later converted to T.7s by Avions Fairey SA at Gosselies. The T.7s served with No.40 Sqn of the Operational Training Unit at Coxyde. The Royal Netherlands Air Force also acquired 10 T.7s, including the prototype, G-AKPK, and all of these were turned over in 1957 to the Royal Netherlands Naval Air Service to provide conversion training for the Dutch Navy's Hawker Sea Hawk FGA.6s. The T.7s and Sea Hawks equipped No.3 Sqn at Valkenburg Air Base, a second Sea Hawk squadron based here being No.860, and the T.7s had the Dutch Navy serials 131 to 140, although not all of these were taken up. The Royal Danish Air Force had five Meteor T.7s as well as 20 F.4s on its formation on 1 October 1950, and four more T.7s were added to the inventory, these remaining in service until 1963.

The Egyptian Air Force acquired six Meteor T.7s to supplement its 12 F.4s, and in 1953 the Israeli Defence Forces/Air Force received its first combat jets when 11 Meteor F.8s and four T.7s were delivered; several more T.7s were later acquired in Belgium. But when in 1955 Egypt and Czechoslovakia signed an agreement for the supply of further arms, the Israelis placed an initial order in France for 24 Dassault Mystère IIC (later Mk IVA) jet fighters to supplement the Dassault M.D.450 Ouragan jets already ordered, as the Meteors were now becoming obsolescent and would be outclassed by the MiG-15s in Egyptian Air Force service. Nine Meteor P.R.9s and six N.F.13s had also been supplied to

the Israeli Air Force, but after the 1956 Sinai campaign it was decided to rely solely on France for further combat aircraft, as it was felt that Britain and the USA could not be relied upon to continue supplies in the face of Arab political pressures. In 1962 the Israeli Air Force's old training sequence, starting with the Boeing-Stearman PT-17 Kaydet for basic training and going on to the Harvard for advanced training and the Meteor T.7 for jet conversion, was replaced by a new one in which Piper Cubs and Super Cubs were used for basic training, going on to the Israeli-built Potez-Air Fouga CM.170 Magister jet trainer and the Dassault Ouragan for operational training. These now replaced the Meteor T.7s, which were henceforth gradually retired.

During 1953-55 the Fôrça Aérea Brasileira took delivery of 60 Meteor F.8s and 10 T.7s, and by 1966 the survivors of these were still equipping the 1° Grupo de Aviação de Caça and the 14° Grupo de Aviação de Caça, based at the Santa Cruz and Canoas Air Force Bases, and with a statutory strength of two and one squadrons respectively. Budgetary restrictions, and the greater priority attached to the Brazilian Air Force's internal communications duties with transport aircraft, meant that the Meteors were not finally replaced by more modern types such as the Dassault Mirage IIIE until the 1970s had dawned. The Royal Australian Air Force's No.77 Sqn used four Meteor T.7s to convert its Mustang pilots to the Meteor F.8 at Iwakuni in Japan from the end of May 1951; the F.8s were used mostly on ground attack duties in Korea until December 1954. The T.7s used for No.77's conversions were serialled A77-229, -305, -380 and -577, and were later reserialled A77-701 to A77-704 respectively; three more RAAF T.7s were serialled A77-705 to A77-707. The first production T.7, VW410, had been delivered to the RAAF as A77-2 in February

1952 for use by the Aircraft Research and Development Unit, and was followed by a second T.7 for the Unit, A77-4 (ex-WN321), in December 1953. The RAAF had also operated a few T.7s with the Vampire F.B.9s of No.78 Wing on garrison duty in Malta, flying from RNAS Hal Far from August 1952 to 1955. The RAAF's last T.7, A77-702, was retired in May 1963 and became a 'gate guardian' at RAAF Laverton, Victoria.

A two-seater demonstration and photographic Meteor was produced in 1954 by fitting a Meteor T.7 cockpit and front fuselage to the now demilitarised PV ground attack prototype of the Meteor F.8 with the Class B registration G-7-1, which first flew in this form on 9 August 1951. This became the Meteor P.V.7-8 G-ANSO, and its Certificate of Airworthiness was issued on 9 July 1954; it was fitted with two wing tip tanks instead of the more usual underwing kind. After several years of use by Gloster's it was sold in August 1959 to the Swedish firm Svensk Flygtjanst AB (or Swedish Air Service Ltd) of Bromma Airport, Stockholm, for conversion to a target tug and use on their extensive target-towing

services for the Swedish and Danish armed forces; the firm also did some air charter work and aerial surveys, and G-ANSO was sold to them as SE-DCC. Svensk Flygtjanst had earlier acquired two Meteor T.7s, WF833 and WA128, for use as target tugs, these becoming SE-CAS and SE-CAT and being delivered in July 1955 and March 1956 respectively. SE-CAT was lost in an accident at Visby on 21 January 1959. Later four Meteor T.T.20s were leased from the Danish Air Force as SE-DCF, SE-DCG, SE-DCH and SE-DCI.

Above: Now one of the RAF's 'Vintage Pair' Meteor T.7s, WA669 is seen here coded '27' when it served with the Tactical Weapons Unit at Brawdy in Wales.

Below: When fitted with the cockpits and forward fuselage of a T.7, the former PV ground attack prototype Meteor F.8 G-7-1 became G-ANSO. It was finished in larkspur blue all over, with ivory registration letters, fuselage flash and wing tip tanks. It was sold to Svensk Flygtjänst AB in 1959 as SE-DCC for target towing.

The Meteor Trainer

Right: Close up of the forward cockpit of one of the 'Vintage Pair' Meteor T.7s; among the instruments visible in the top row are the Machmeter (extreme left), airspeed indicator, artificial horizon and (top right) two engine rpm counters.

Below right: This view of the Meteor T.7 rear cockpit shows full dual control and a slight rearrangement of instruments, the two engine rev counters being at the top of the panel. Note striped cockpit hood jettison handle on the right.

Below left: This view shows both cockpits and how the canopy opens sideways. On the centre coaming is the vhf radio on the left and the accelerometer or g indicator on the right.

The Meteor Test-Beds

The F.9/40 prototypes had performed a valuable service as test-beds for the early British jet engines, and later Meteor variants were to continue this service for post-war British turbojet developments, right up to deflected jet thrust and lift engines for the VTOL era. The pioneer work on reheat started with Meteor F.I EE215 was continued by two Meteor F.4s, RA435 and VT196, which were fitted respectively with Derwent 5 and 8 engines modified by Rolls-Royce to have reheat; the jet pipes on RA435 when it appeared at the 1949 SBAC Display at Farnborough were seen to be noticeably longer than those of the standard F.4. This reheat installation gave a 25 per cent increase in thrust but at a cost of 900 gals/h (4,091 litres/h) in fuel consumption. A variable-area jet pipe nozzle was featured, and a major difficulty of reheat installations at that time was finding nozzle and jet pipe wall materials that would stand up to the intense heat of afterburning. Some 500 hours of development flying were accumulated on the three reheat Meteors before the major part of reheat development shifted to the Avon. Following on the earlier installation of two Metrovick F.2s in the F.9/40 prototype DG204/G, which became the first British axial-flow engines to fly, on 13 November 1943, Meteor F.4 RA490 was fitted with two 3,950-lb (1,792-kg) s.t. (maximum take-off) Metrovick F.2/4 Beryl 1 turbojets, this engine having the Ministry of Supply designation MVB.3, and two of them also being fitted in the Saunders-Roe SR/A1 flying boat fighter. Whereas the F.2/1s in the F.9/40 DG204/G were underslung from the wings, as they were too long to fit between the spars, the Beryls in RA490 were mounted under a curved, inverted U-section

Bottom: Meteor F.4 RA435 was modified by Rolls-Royce to have reheat in its Derwent 5 engines, with noticeably longer jet pipes than the standard ones. This reheat gave a 25 per cent thrust increase but at some cost in fuel consumption.

Below: Meteor F.4 RA491 was the most powerful single-seater aeroplane in the world when it first appeared in 1949 with two RA.2 Avons of over 6,000 lb (2,725 kg) s.t. each. In April 1950 it first flew with slightly more powerful RA.3 Avons.

incorporated in both front and rear spars; this gave them a lower thrust line than the Derwent 5s but still gave sufficient ground clearance when longer type undercarriage units were used, as had been employed in the F.9/40 DG204/G. Similarly modified spars were used for the Avon installation in F.4 RA491, and the Beryl nacelles of RA490 were slightly longer than the Derwent ones. Both the Beryl- and Avon-powered Meteors had fantastic rates of climb; at a loaded weight of 15,455 lb (7,010 kg) the Beryl-Meteor reached 10,000 ft (3,048 m)

in 55 seconds; 20,000 ft (6,000 m) in 2 minutes, 5 seconds; 30,000 ft (9,144 m) in 3 minutes, 43 seconds; and 40,000 ft (12,192 m) in 7 minutes, 31 seconds. Although a promising engine, development of the Beryl was overshadowed and eventually superseded by that of an even larger and more powerful axial-flow engine known as the Metrovick F.9 Sapphire, and further development of this was taken over by Armstrong Siddeley Motors Ltd in 1948 after Metropolitan-Vickers had decided to pull out of the aero engine field.

Meteor F.4 RA491 was fitted with two Rolls-Royce RA.2 Avons of over 6,000 lb (2,721 kg) s.t. (maximum take-off) each, which when it first appeared in 1949 made it the most powerful single-seater aeroplane in the world. The Avon installation was similar to that of RA490, the nacelles being of larger diameter and extending further forward than the Derwent ones. Flown by Wing Commander J. H. Heyworth, assistant chief test pilot of Rolls-Royce, at the 1949 SBAC Show, RA491 put on a memorable display in which Heyworth extinguished both Avons together and re-lit them after doing an upward roll, to demonstrate the Avon's considerable power. In April 1950 RA491 first flew with two 6,500-lb (2,948-kg) s.t. RA.3 Avons, this variant differing from the RA.2 Avon in having a two-stage instead of a single-stage turbine, as well as various improvements to the compressor and turbine blades made in the course of RA.2 development. The RA.3 Avon went into large-scale production for the Canberra, and with these engines RA491 climbed to 40,000 ft (12,192 m) in 2.7 minutes and to 50,000 ft (15,240 m) in the incredible time of 3.65 minutes.

In 1954 the Beryl-Meteor RA490 was modified by Westland Aircraft Ltd for jet deflection experiments, for which it was fitted with two RN.4 Nene turbojets with jet deflectors exhausting downwards

under the nacelles. These engines had to be mounted forward of the front spars so that the deflected jets' thrust component could pass through the region of the centre of gravity. Very large nacelles were featured, extending about 8 ft (2.4 m) forward of the front spars, an F.8 tail unit was fitted, as well as endplate fins on the tailplane, and the wing span was increased to 44 ft 4 in (13.51 m). Flight trials were successful, and jet deflection enabled a minimum air speed of 65 knots (115 km/h) to be achieved, although at some cost in complexity. This was an important step on the road that eventually led to the Hawker P.1127 Kestrel and Harrier. The Avon-Meteor RA491 was later sold to the French SNECMA aero engine company, who used it as a test bed for the SNECMA Atar 101 turbojet, and its new owners also fitted it with a Meteor F.8 front fuselage, amongst many other modifications.

In August 1950, Meteor F.8 WA820 flew with two 7,600-lb (3,447-kg) s.t. Armstrong Siddeley ASSa.2 Sapphire turbojets, this installation being made by another Hawker-Siddeley Group company, Air Service Training Ltd at Hamble, and necessitating extensive strengthening and modifications to the airframe. The Sapphire-Meteor now took over from the Avon-Meteor the claim to be the most powerful single-seater aeroplane in the world, and in theory it could have exceeded its limiting Mach number in level flight on one engine. On 31 August 1951, flown by Flt Lt R. B. Prickett, it set a time-to-height record of 3 minutes 7 seconds to 12,000 m (39,370 ft) from a standing start; this record stood for several years.

Flight testing of the more powerful ASSa.6 and ASSa.7 Sapphires was done in Canberra B.2 WD933, as the engine was now too powerful for the Meteor airframe.

Another Meteor F.8, VZ517, was used by Rolls-Royce at Hucknall for investigating the problem of engine surge in the Derwent 8, and later, in 1955, was fitted with an Armstrong Siddeley ASSc.2-1 Screamer rocket engine under the fuselage. The single combustion chamber of this engine was angled downwards at 10° to take the rocket efflux clear of the fuselage, the underside of the rear fuselage being skinned with stainless steel separated from the original metal skin by an 0.5-in air gap. The Screamer used as propellants a combination of liquid oxygen, wide-cut aviation gasoline and water; the fuel and water tanks were accommodated in the fuselage, and the liquid oxygen was contained in a complex design of double-bubble tank mounted immediately forward of the rocket motor itself. The whole was neatly faired in to form a long streamlined nacelle and, to avoid having to make a belly landing on the liquid oxygen tank, this was arranged to be jettisonable in an emergency. The Screamer developed a static thrust of up to 8,000 lb (3,629 kg) at sea level, the thrust being controllable, but the engine never went into production because of official disfavour with the propellant combination used. Later the 1957 Defence White Paper led to the cancellation of mixed powerplant rocket/jet

Meteor F.R.9 VZ608 was fitted with a Rolls-Royce RB.108 lift engine installed vertically in the centre fuselage to evaluate this type of installation.

interceptors such as the Saunders-Roe SR.177 and Avro 720, and put paid to further development of British rocket engines for manned military aircraft.

At the 1954 SBAC Display the first of a new generation of small Rolls-Royce jet engines was revealed, giving great power for their size, and thus suitable for such applications as lift engines (in multiple clutches) for VTOL aircraft, or singly as target drone engines. This was the 1,810-lb (821-kg) s.t. RB.82 or RSr.2 Soar, one of which was bolted through its monocoque casing to each wing tip of Meteor F.8 WA982, without any cowling at all; this increased the span to 39 ft 10 in (12.1 m). At the time it first appeared, the Soar delivered more thrust per unit weight – its total weight was 275 lb (125 kg) – and frontal area than any other air-breathing engine. The Soar developed more thrust than the Welland I of the Meteor F.I, but had a diameter of only 15.75 in (40 cm). It was built under licence in the States by Westinghouse as the J81 for the Radioplane XQ-4 supersonic drone, but it was soon superseded in this country by new small high-power turbojets such as the RB.108, RB.145 and RB.162. Meteor F.R.9 VZ608 was fitted with an RB.108 lift engine installed vertically in the centre fuselage, and was used for intake and engine-mounting tests to establish the characteristics of a lift engine installation. Because the RB.108 displaced the main fuel tank, two 100-gal (454-litres) underwing

Bottom: This view of Meteor F.R.9 VZ608 shows a flush dorsal intake for the centrally-mounted RB.108 ; the armament has been removed.

drop tanks were carried. The Short SC.1 VTOL research delta, which first flew in April 1957, had four RB.108 lift engines plus a fifth fitted in the tail for normal forward propulsion.

In France the SFECMAS S.600 ramjet (its designation came from the internal duct diameter of 600 mm) was flight tested, at first mounted under the port wing of a Junkers Ju 88G, and later under the starboard wing of a French Air Force Meteor N.F.11 serialled NF11-3. The S.600 had a maximum sea level thrust at 621 mph (1,000 km/h) of 1,320 lb (599 kg). The privately-owned SFECMAS (Société Francaise d'Etudes et de Contructions de Matériels Aéronautiques Speciaux) was taken over late in 1954 by the State-owned SNCA du Nord, and Nord continued testing the S.600 under the Meteor for several years after.

Perhaps the most interesting experimental Meteor of all was WK935, the last of 430 F.8s to be built by Armstrong Whitworth, which was modified by them to evaluate the prone pilot position for the Institute of Aviation Medicine, and also for its proposed use in the Bristol Type 185 rocket-

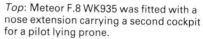

Top: Meteor F.8 WK935 was fitted with a nose extension carrying a second cockpit for a pilot lying prone.

powered interceptor project. The chief advantage of this arrangement was that a pilot lying on his stomach would not black out in tight turns because, in the prone position, blood would not drain from the head as it would when the pilot was sitting upright. A tapering nose section about 8 ft (2.4 m) long was fitted to WK935 ahead of the normal cockpit, increasing the length to 52 ft 5 in (15.98 m) and this accommodated the pilot prone on a padded bed, with his head slightly up and knees partially bent. A second cockpit canopy was fitted at the end of this section, the controls being duplicated in the normal cockpit, and a safety pilot was always carried when the aircraft was being flown prone. To bale out, the prone pilot's bed, and its supporting floor, was hinged downwards at the forward end so that the pilot would slide off the bed feet first and fall away from the aircraft. WK935 first flew in prone-pilot form from Baginton in February 1954 and continued trials until the end of 1955. These showed that while there was no special difficulty in operating the controls while lying prone, pilots found it difficult to look sideways or backwards, and 'g' forces acting in unaccustomed directions could cause discomfort. In the end, the prone pilot concept was overtaken by the development of the anti-g pressure suit for fighter pilots.

The Meteor F.8

A major redesign of the Meteor F.4, to improve its performance and to correct the inherent tail heaviness that had resulted in the F.4 carrying over 1,000 lb (454 kg) of ballast forward, resulted in the G.41P Meteor F.8, which retained as many F.4 components as possible for ease of production. Progressive strengthening of earlier marks of Meteor, increases in the engine weight and the addition of more equipment in the rear fuselage had necessitated the F.4 carrying up to 1,095 lb (497 kg) of ballast in the form of lead weights attached to the nosewheel mounting structure, and to the use of heavy alloy rings to form the engine intake leading edges. As related in an earlier chapter, Meteor F.4 RA382 had been fitted with a 30-in (76-cm) forward fuselage extension inserted at the front spar bulkhead joint, and on production F.8s this extra space was used to house a 95-Imp gal (432-litres) fuel tank. This fuselage 'plug' moved the cannon and 800 lb (363 kg) of ammunition further forward, which caused some problems on RA382 because as the guns were fired the nose became lighter.

A larger tail unit was really needed, and it was found by tests in the RAE wind tunnel that fitting the tail of the Gloster GA.2 or E.1/44 single-seater fighter to the Meteor F.4 would admirably restore longitudinal control. This was accordingly fitted to RA382, and proved to be an instant success, so it was made a standard feature of the F.8; the upper component of the E.1/44's fin was made of wood to take a suppressed radio aerial, but on the F.8 this part was replaced by metal. The E.1/44, sometimes known as the Ace, was designed around a single 5000-lb (2,268-kg) s.t. Nene 2 turbojet, but did not go into production. The first prototype, SM 809, was damaged beyond repair while being transported to Boscombe Down by road in August 1947 for its first flight; the second prototype, TX145, first flew at Boscombe on 9 March 1948 piloted by 'Bill' Waterton, and was followed by a third prototype, TX148.

The second prototype Meteor F.8 was VT150 which, as related in an earlier chapter, was built as an F.4 and used for the trial installation of the Martin-Baker Mk 1E ejector seat, which made it necessary to move the windscreen forward and to fit a completely new one-piece electrically-operated cockpit hood, amongst other modifications. VT150 later had the F.8 tail unit and forward fuselage 'plug', first flying in this form on 12 October 1948. It was later used for testing anti-spin parachute installations for the Javelin all-weather fighter, and also for investigating the effect of gun blast on the surrounding nose structure. The Martin-Baker Mk 1E seat was standard in the Meteor F.8, and these seats were later converted to Mk 2E fully-automatic standards, afterwards being further modified to have the Duplex drogue system to bring the minimum safe ejection height down to 125 ft (38 m). The F.8 also had uprated RD.7 Derwent 8 engines of 3,600 lb (1,633 kg) s.t. each, and later production aircraft had larger engine intakes, spring tab ailerons and a modified cockpit canopy.

Flight tests soon showed the Meteor F.8 to be a great improvement over earlier marks, the new tail improving control at high speeds and raising the limiting Mach number to 0.82, while general handling qualities were easy. An initial batch of 128 F.8s were ordered, and altogether 1,183 of this mark were built, 430 of them by Armstrong Whitworth at Baginton, near Coventry. The first F.8 to be delivered to an RAF unit was VZ440, which joined No. 43 (F) Sqn on 2 August 1949 at Tangmere in Sussex, and the first

The second prototype Meteor F.8 VT150 started life as an F.4 and was used for the trial installation of the Martin-Baker Mk 1E ejector seat.

production F.8, VZ438, joined No. 1(F) Sqn, also at Tangmere, on 10 December that year. The latter F.8 was later used at Farnborough to develop the F.R.9, and was fitted with an F.R.9 camera nose, before finally being converted to a T.T.8 target tug. In this form it tested a new radar-reflecting target streamed from a pod under the starboard wing.

The first squadron to re-equip completely with F.8s was No. 245 at Horsham St Faith, Norfolk, which used this mark from 29 June 1950 to March 1957; this unit also had the last F.8 in RAF service, which left in April 1957 after the squadron converted to Hunter F.4s in March that year, only to be disbanded three months later. The last F.8 to be built, WL191, left the Gloster factory on 9 April 1954. In 1951, No. 245's Meteor F.8s took part in probe and drogue in-flight refuelling trials to see for how long fighters could be kept airborne in this way for standing patrols, and altogether 13 F.8s were fitted with a nose probe that transferred fuel to the main fuselage tank. These were the first flight-refuelling trials to be carried out by an RAF squadron, and they proved that six Meteors could be kept flying for 3-4 hours at a stretch. Altogether Meteor F.8s equipped no less than 20 regular and 10 Royal Auxiliary Air Force squadrons, as well as No. 211 Advanced Flying School and No. 266 Operational Conversion Unit; in most cases F.8s replaced F.4s in the squadron. The 10 Auxiliary squadrons all continued to fly their F.8s right up to the disbandment of the Royal Auxiliary Air Force on 10 March 1957.

Left: Three Meteor F.8s of No 500 (County of Kent) Sqn, Royal Auxiliary Air Force.

Right: The second PV ground attack Meteor F.8 prototype G-7-1, also known as the Reaper, is seen here with twenty-four 65-lb (29-kg) rocket projectiles.

After the F.8 had left first-line service a number were converted to Meteor T.T.8 target tugs by the addition of a target-towing lug to the ventral tank; because there was no internal stowage for the target and no winch was fitted for streaming it in flight, it was attached to the towing lug before take-off and dropped just before landing. T.T.8s had the black and yellow diagonal undersurfaces of target-towing aircraft. The last Meteor to serve with the Far East Air Force was T.T.8 WH398 which was retired from the Towed Target Flight at Seletar, Singapore, at the end of 1961. A number of F.8s were also converted to single-seat advanced trainers as Meteor T.8s, WH301 being one of the first to be modified. The F.8 could also be converted into a Meteor F.R.9 by fitting the camera nose of that mark, but only one F.8, VZ438 mentioned earlier, was so fitted, all the F.R.9s being built as such.

A number of Meteor F.8s were used for various experimental jobs and trial installations. VZ439 was fitted with an experimental strengthened hood for operations at high altitude, this being largely opaque with two circular windows on each side. VZ442 was used to find a satisfactory solution to the problem of faulty canopy fastenings, while VZ460 was used for bomb, bomb pylon and rocket projectile tests at the Central Fighter Establishment. It was also flown with spring tab ailerons, these also being tested on F.8 WH843; these ailerons, fitted on later production F.8s, gave an improved rate of roll and reduced lateral stick forces at high speed. At the 1950 SBAC Display, F.8

WA878 gave an aerobatic display carrying a 1,000-lb (453-kg) bomb under each wing, as well as a ventral tank, while displayed statically was Gloster's private venture ground attack Meteor F.8 G-AMCJ, modified from a standard F.8. This had first flown on 4 September 1950, and featured some local strengthening in the fuselage, as well as a stronger undercarriage – the same as on the Meteor N.F.11 – to cater for the much greater weight of external 'stores' that could be carried.

G-AMCJ had provision for two 20-mm or 30-mm cannon in a streamlined under-fuselage pack, four 1,000-lb (453-kg) bombs (two under the wings and two under the fuselage), up to 16 96-lb (43.5-kg) rocket projectiles under the wings in tiers of four and up to eight under the fuselage (two were actually fitted there), and two 100-Imp gal (454-litres) underwing drop tanks, two tanks of the same capacity on the wing tips as well as the standard ventral tank. Various combinations of these bombs, rockets and drop tanks could have been carried, and G-AMCJ was also stressed for the use of jettisonable RATOG (Rocket-Assisted Take-Off Gear), each RATO unit giving 1,500-lb (680-kg) thrust for six seconds; this was intended for shorter take-offs at high weights from land bases, rather than aircraft carrier decks, and some thought was also given to the fitting of an arrestor hook to this variant, also for use from land bases. The dummy wing tip tanks fitted increased the span to 41 ft (12.5 m), but this Meteor did not have the necessarily strengthened wing, and never flew as a ground attack aeroplane. G-AMCJ was finished dark red all over, with cream registration letters, fuselage

flash and lettering; some of the 'stores' displayed around it were also painted in cream. This Meteor was sold to the Danish Air Force in February 1951 with the serial '490'.

A second similar PV ground attack variant of the Meteor F.8, also known as the Gloster G.44 Reaper, was built with the Class B registration G-7-1, and was shown at the 1951 SBAC Display at Farnborough carrying 24 96-lb (43.5-kg) rocket projectiles – eight under each wing in two tiers of four, and eight under the fuselage, also in two tiers; two 100-Imp gal (454-litres) wing tip fuel tanks were fitted and, carrying these 'stores', G-7-1 gave a spectacular aerobatic display. Four 1,000-lb (453-kg) bombs could also have been carried in place of the rockets, two under the wings and two under the fuselage. As related in a previous chapter, this Meteor was later fitted with a T.7 cockpit and front fuselage and became G-ANSO.

Several more Meteor F.8s were employed experimentally, VZ500 being used to investigate the effect of yaw on an autostabiliser, and VZ567 to investigate and find a cure for the problem of spent cartridge cases falling against and damaging the ventral tank. F.8 WA775 was used to test the nose radar for D.H. Firestreak air-to-air missiles fitted on Hawker Hunters, while WE855 was used in 1957 for a series of experiments testing over-run 'catch' barriers on airfields. At least five Meteor F.8s were fitted with an Irving brake parachute in a small pack on the port side of the rear fuselage.

The Meteor F.8 overseas

The Meteor F.8 was exported to most of the countries that had ordered the F.4, and also to Australia, Brazil, Syria and Israel. The Belgian Air Force acquired a batch of 23 ex-RAF F.8s, serialled EG-201 to EG-223, prior to the second batch of 150 F.8s, with serials EG-1 to EG-150, which were assembled by Avions Fairey SA at Gosselies from components made and supplied by Fokker, these being part of the 348 Meteor F.8s built by the Dutch aircraft company for the Belgian and Netherlands Air Forces. A third and fourth batch of 30 and 31 F.8s respectively followed, these also being assembled by Avions Fairey from Fokker-built components. The F.8s entered service in 1951, and equipped Nos. 349, 350 and 4 Squadrons of the 1st Wing, Nos. 7, 8 and 9 Squadrons of the 7th Wing, Nos. 22 and 26 Squadrons of the 9th Wing, and Nos. 25, 29, and 33 Squadrons of the 13th Wing, as well as an Operational Training Unit. The F.8s began to be replaced by Hunter F.4s in 1956, and a few of those made obsolete were converted into target tugs similar to the T.T.8 for use at Solenzaru in Corsica, where Belgian squadrons did their air-to-air gunnery training.

The Royal Netherlands Air Force received its first Meteor F.8s when eight ex-RAF aircraft were delivered in July 1951, the first five of these being serialled I-90 to I-94. These were followed by a further 155 Meteor F.8s built under licence by NV Koninklijke Nederlandse Vliegtuigenfabriek Fokker, or Royal Netherlands Aircraft Factories Fokker, to give its full title. The Derwent 8 turbojets were built under licence by the Belgian armaments firm Fabrique

Nationale d'Armes de Guerre SA at Herstal, the first Belgian-built Derwent finishing tests on 21 February 1951, and they had delivered over 1,000 Derwents when production ceased in 1955 in favour of Rolls-Royce Avons for Fokker-built Hunter F.4s and F.6s. On 27 March 1953 the Dutch Air Force became an independent service, equal to the Army and Navy in status, and was known as Koninklijke Luchtmacht, which means 'Royal Air Force' in Dutch. The Meteor F.8s equipped Nos. 322, 323, 324, 325, 326, 327 and 328 Squadrons, and began to be replaced by Hunter F.4s and F.6s from 1956.

In October 1950, 20 Meteor F.8s were ordered for the Royal Danish Air Force, the first of these being delivered in January 1951; they were serialled 481 to 500, and were finished in grey and green camouflage, with natural aluminium undersurfaces. They equipped Eskadrille 724 (No. 724 Sqn) and served until replaced by 30 Hunter F.51s during 1956-57, the last F.8 being phased out in 1963. The Brazilian Air Force, or Fôrça Aérea Brasileira took delivery of 60 Meteor F.8s during 1953-55, these being serialled 4400 to 4459, with black serials on an overall silver finish. As related in an earlier chapter, by 1966 the survivors of these were still equipping the 1° Grupo de Aviacão de Caça and the 14° Grupo de Aviacão de Caça, or 1st and 14th Fighter Groups, stationed at the Santa Cruz and Canoas Air Force bases. Largely because a greater priority was accorded to transport aircraft for internal communications, the Meteor F.8s remained in service almost until the 1970s arrived and Dassault Mirage IIIEBRs were finally ordered for 1972 delivery to re-equip the Fighter Groups.

The Egyptian Air Force ordered 19 Meteor F.8s in October 1949,

Fokker-built Meteor F.8 I-189 of the Royal Netherlands Air Force, which flew with Nos 322 and 326 Squadrons.

plus a further five in December that year, but work on both these contracts had to be suspended a year later following another embargo placed on the sale of arms to Middle Eastern countries. Seven ex-RAF F.8s were delivered to Egypt in December 1952, plus a further 15 supplied three years later. Two of these F.8s were destroyed in the Suez campaign of 1956, but some were still in service in 1958 after the Egyptian Air Force had begun to re-equip with Russian types. Twelve Meteor F.8s for the Syrian Air Force were ordered in 1950 and a dozen RAF F.8s were earmarked for delivery, but following the arms embargo of 1951 these went to RAF squadrons after all. The Syrians eventually took delivery of their F.8s, these being serialled 101 to 112 and camouflaged light earth and green on the upper surfaces, with sky blue under surfaces and white serials. Seven more ex-RAF F.8s were acquired in 1956, two of these being serialled 480 and 481 and the rest not given numbers. Syria's turbulent domestic politics, in which coup had succeeded coup regularly since 1949, made it difficult for their Air Force to realise its full combat potential, especially as numbers of Air Force personnel were arrested in successive political purges. The Syrians used their Meteors largely for ground attack work.

Eleven Meteor F.8s were ordered in 1953 for the Israeli Defence Forces/Air Force and the Israelis supplied the cannon for these aircraft, which were modified to take American 5-in HVAR (High Velocity Aircraft Rocket) rocket projectiles. These F.8s were also modified for use as target tugs, and were serialled 2166 to 2169 and 2172 to 2178; they were delivered finished silver all over,

A formation of Syrian Air Force Meteor F.8s, of which Syria eventually acquired 19.

but were camouflaged after arrival. However, the Meteors were already obsolescent, and would soon be outclassed by the Egyptian Air Force MiG-15s, so the Israelis ordered 24 Dassault Mystère IIC (later Mk IVA) jet fighters to supplement the M.D.450 Ouragans already ordered. Eventually 60 Mystères and 75 Ouragans were supplied, the Mystères first seeing action during the 1956 Sinai campaign, and as they replaced the F.8s in first-line service the latter were used for operational training.

The Meteor F.8 became the first British fighter to fly in real combat since the end of World War II when it was taken into action by the Royal Australian Air Force's No.77 Sqn in Korea. This unit was based at Iwakuni in Japan, 450 miles west of Tokyo on the Inland Sea and under No.81 Wing as part of the British Commonwealth Occupation Force, when a North Korean army crossed the 38th parallel into South Korea on 25 June 1950 and the Korean War began. No.77 was equipped with Mustangs, both Commonwealth CA-17 and CA-18 variants built in Australia and P-51Ds. On 30 June Mr Robert Menzies, the Australian Prime Minister, offered No.77 Sqn for service in Korea, and on 2 July the squadron flew its first operational sortie of the campaign when it provided escort for USAF B-29 Superfortresses attacking the North Korean airfield of Yongpu. On 4 May 1951, No.77 returned to Iwakuni from Pusan with its Mustangs to convert to the Meteor F.8, of which 15 had been ferried out from Renfrew in Scotland in February, picketed on the flight deck of the carrier H.M.S. *Warrior*; two Meteor T.7s were also on the ship, these being A77-229 and A77-305. A further 20 F.8s were

similarly ferried out to Iwakuni not long after, and four experienced RAF pilots also arrived with this second batch to help the Australians to convert to Meteors; as related earlier, four T.7s were used for conversion training at Iwakuni. While this progressed, it was decided that each Meteor must be fitted with a radio compass before returning to Korea, but this did not prove to be possible and only one ARN-6 radio compass-equipped aircraft was provided for each flight of F.8s, which flew to a minimum cloud base of 1,000 ft (305 m). The radio compass loop was incorporated in the aerial mast mounting, and was covered by a small Perspex blister made in Australia.

On 30 June 1951, No.77 Sqn moved to Kimpo in Korea, and the first operational mission was flown on 30 July when 16 Meteor F.8s carried out a high altitude sweep in the vicinity of the Yalu river in company with USAF F-86 Sabres. The first few sweeps and escort missions met no real opposition, but on 29 August eight Meteors carrying out a sweep over Chongju in the notorious 'MiG alley' at 37,000 ft (11,277 m) sighted over 30 Chinese Air Force MiG-15s at 45,000 ft (13,716 m). One Meteor was shot down, the pilot baling out and becoming a prisoner of war. Sqn Ldr Wilson, who was leading the formation, was on the tail of a MiG and flying at Mach 0.84 when his Meteor was hit from above and below. His port aileron was made ineffective but he returned to Kimpo and made a successful landing at 30 knots above normal landing speed; no MiG was claimed as a confirmed 'kill'. On 5 September six Meteors were escorting USAF RF-80 Shooting Stars on a photo recce mission in the Antung area and were flying at 20,000 ft (6,096 m) when they were attacked by a dozen MiGs. In the ensuing dogfight, lasting five or six minutes, W/O Michelson, flying F.8 A77-726, was 'bounced' by three MiGs and suffered quite

considerable damage before finally shaking them off. He escaped with a 2-ft (61-cm) diameter hole in the port tailplane, considerable damage between the port engine and the fuselage and a damaged starboard aileron, with the trim tab hanging by one hinge.

No MiGs were claimed shot down in this action, nor on another escort mission on 26 September for RF-80 Shooting Stars, when 12 Meteors were attacked by over 30 MiGs. Again, one F.8 was damaged but Flt Lt Dawson flying another Meteor, chased a MiG and got in a few good bursts at it; pieces were seen coming off the wing, but the cine camera record of this 'probable' turned out to be over-exposed. On 24 October, 16 Meteors in four sections were escorting B-29 Superfortresses to bomb Sunchon when they ran into a dogfight between F-86 Sabres and MiGs; at first they could not fire for fear of hitting a Sabre, but later managed to get in a few bursts. Fg Off Hamilton-Foster's Meteor was badly damaged, and his starboard engine flamed out as he was descending, but he managed to land safely at base. Sadly, six MiGs were able to break through the Meteors and shoot down a B-29.

Although the Australian pilots were superior, it was clear that the Meteor F.8 was outclassed by the MiG-15, being much slower and lacking manoeuvrability at height. It also lacked adequate rear view because of the dural structure at the rear of the cockpit canopy, although a fully transparent cockpit hood was later fitted to RAF F.8s. For a time No.77's Meteors fulfilled the role of escorts to the B-29s, but the USAF finally abandoned daylight B-29 raids because of the losses they suffered. The Chinese MiGs operated from safe bases in Manchuria, the former Japanese puppet-state under Chinese rule since 1945 which shared a border with North Korea. Meanwhile, work was resumed on adapting the

The Meteor F. 8 overseas

Meteor to the ground attack role, which had been put aside because of the escort commitments. 'Stores' pylons, based on the type carried by the USAF F-80 Shooting Stars, were fitted with an American electrical release system, this system being attached to the Meteor's tank release slip. Possible loads of two 500-lb (227-kg) or two 1,000-lb (453-kg) bombs were considered, and two napalm tanks were also fitted. A rocket projectile with a 6½-gallon (29.5-litres) napalm warhead was also developed for the Meteor, but this provided insufficient napalm to be effective.

On 27 October Fg Off Reading severely damaged a MiG and several other pilots scored hits, while on 2 November during a dogfight between 16 Meteors and a large number of MiGs Flt Lt Joe Blythe again damaged a MiG. He later said that he could have hit more, but his windscreen had recently been changed and he had previously used one of the cracks in the old one to sight MiGs at 800 yards (730 m). A third MiG was damaged the following day by a pilot named Colebrook; two Meteors were also damaged in this action but were able to return to base, although one of these was sufficiently badly damaged by cannon fire – and the subsequent successful wheels-up landing – to be broken up for spares. On 1 December, 12 Meteors on a sweep at 19,000 ft (5,791 m) tangled with over 50 MiGs north of Pyongyang; at last the squadron's first confirmed MiG 'kill' was scored in the ensuing dogfight by Fg Off Bruce Gogerly, flying F.8 A77-17. A second confirmed MiG was hit by a

number of pilots, and so was credited to the squadron as a 'kill' rather than to any individual. But two Meteors failed to return after apparently being 'jumped' by MiGs as they were leaving the combat area and a third, flown by Sgt Thomson, had R/T failure after asking for a course to steer and crashed on its way back to base after finally running out of fuel. This left the squadron with only 14 serviceable Meteors, which was considered too few to maintain a squadron effort; No.77 was then detailed to carry out area defence and airfield defence at Kimpo and Suwon against possible MiG attacks on fighter bases, and in these roles the Meteor's superior rate of climb to the F-86 Sabre could be employed to advantage.

But the squadron's new CO, Wing Commander Ronald Susans, who arrived at the end of December 1951, was not content with a purely defensive role. He sought and successfully obtained permission for the Meteors to be used in the ground attack role, even though the type had not been cleared by the RAF for use with rocket projectiles. The CO himself led the first ground attack sortie on 8 January 1952 against the water tower at Chongdan, which was successful even though only cannon fire was used. During January, No.77 flew 769 ground attack sorties, and over 1,000 such sorties in February. These missions could be much more dangerous than air-to-air combat because of accurate ground fire and nine Meteors were lost in these sorties in the first five months of 1952. Eight 60-lb (27-kg) rocket projectiles or two 500-lb (227-kg) bombs were usually carried under the wings in this role. Some escort work was still undertaken, as on 4 May 1952 when the squadron provided cover for USAF fighter-bombers, and encountered some MiGs five miles

from Pyongyang, the North Korean capital. Pilot Officer John Surman fired a good burst at a MiG and saw it go down without taking any evasive action, but he could claim only a 'possible' as he did not actually see it crash. Four days later, Fg Off Bill Simmonds shot down another MiG, also in a dogfight near Pyongyang, but this time the 'kill' was definite as several pilots saw the MiG pilot bale out. In May, No.77 began fighter sweeps again, and the last encounter with a MiG was in March 1953 when Sgt John Hale claimed one shot down.

No.77 Sqn continued in action until the cease-fire was declared on 27 July 1953, and in 37 months of the Korean campaign with both Mustangs and Meteors it flew 4,836 missions (or 18,872 individual sorties) and was credited with the destruction of 3,700 buildings, 1,500 vehicles and 16 bridges. In addition, No.77 was credited with three MiGs destroyed by Meteors, and three propeller-driven aircraft by the Mustangs. The squadron lost 42 pilots, 32 of them in Meteors. In December 1954 the squadron returned to Australia on board the carrier HMAS *Vengeance*, which also brought back the Meteors, and No.77 was now based at Williamstown. In 1955 it re-equipped with the CA-26 Avon Sabre Mk 30, the Commonwealth-built Avon-engined version of the F-86E Sabre, and the Meteor F.8s were then relegated to training, some being passed on to two squadrons of the Citizen Air Force, Australia's equivalent of the Royal Auxiliary Air Force. These were No.22 (City of Sydney) Sqn at Richmond, New South Wales, and No.23 (City of Brisbane) Sqn, based at Amberley in Queensland. In June 1960 the Citizen Air Force was changed to a non-flying role. Some F.8s were also used as target tugs. The last RAAF unit with the Meteor F.8s was No. 75 Sqn, which also flew a three-man aerobatic team called 'The Meteorites'.

The Meteor F.R.9, of which the prototype VW360 is seen here, was a tactical reconnaissance variant of the F.8.

Photo Recce and target drone variants

In the early post war years RAF squadrons at home and overseas continued to use variants of the Spitfire and Mosquito for photographic reconnaissance, the Spitfire F.R.18 being used for tactical fighter reconnaissance by the Middle and Far East Air Force squadrons, while the Spitfire P.R.19 and Mosquito P.R.34 were used for longer range photo reconnaissance, especially during the Malayan anti-terrorist campaign. The first photo recce variant of the Meteor, the sole P.R.V, had not gone into production and to replace the Spitfire F.R.18 a tactical reconnaissance variant of the Meteor F.8 designated F.R.9 was produced, the prototype, VW360, making its first flight on 23 March 1950; it was later fitted with four HVAR rocket projectiles under each wing. The F.R.9 retained the armament of four cannon and featured an F.24 camera in the nose on a universal mounting that could be remotely controlled by the pilot to shoot straight ahead or obliquely to port or starboard through three optically flat camera ports in the nose. The first production Meteor F.8, VZ438, had been used to develop the F.R.9's camera nose at Farnborough, and was later converted to a T.T.8 target tug. Two Meteor T.7s, EE530 and WL375, were also fitted with the F.R.9 nose late in their careers, as well as the F.8 tail unit. The last Meteor F.R.9 of 126 built for the RAF, WX981, was delivered on 14 August 1952.

Meteor F.R.9s equipped four squadrons, Nos. 2 and 79 with BAFO and the 2nd Tactical Air Force in Germany, and Nos. 8 and 208 of the Middle East Air Force. No. 2 was the first unit to re-quip with F.R.9s, which began to replace its Spitfire P.R.19s and F.R.14s from December 1950, and were based successively at Buckeburg, Gutersloh, Wahn and Geilenkirchen until replaced by Supermarine Swift F.R.5s from March 1956; the squadron also had a number of Meteor P.R.10s on its strength from March to June 1951. No. 79 Sqn, which had flown Thunderbolt IIs in Burma until disbanded at the end of December 1945, was reformed at Gutersloh on 15 November 1951 as a fighter reconnaissance unit with Meteor F.R.9s which it flew until, like No. 2 Sqn, it also re-equipped with Swift F.R.5s from June 1956.

No. 8 Sqn was based in Aden and was predominantly a Venom F.B.4 unit which had some Meteor F.R.9s on strength from January 1958. On 1 August 1959 the squadron's 'C' Flight, operating the F.R.9s, became the Arabian Peninsula Reconnaissance Flight, but this flight rejoined No. 8 in August 1960. In January that year the squadron had replaced its Venoms with Hunter FGA.9s, and in April 1961 the Meteor F.R.9s were also replaced by Hunters, this time the F.R.10 tactical reconnaissance variant. No. 208 Sqn replaced its Spitfire F.R.18s with Meteor F.R.9s in March 1951 when it was based at Fayid in the Canal Zone, and they remained in service until replaced by Hunter F.5s and F.6s in January 1958; during this time the F.R.9s were also based at Abu Sueir in the Canal Zone and, during 1956, at Hal Far and Takali in Malta and Akrotiri in Cyprus. At home, Meteor F.R.9 WE919 was fitted with underwing rocket launchers, and another F.R.9, VZ608, was used by Rolls Royce to test an RB.108 mounted in the centre fuselage.

Seven Meteor F.R.9s were supplied to the Israeli Air Force during 1954-55, and in September 1955 two of these engaged four Egyptian Air Force Vampire F.B.52s in a dogfight and shot down two of them. The Ecuadorean Air Force, or Fuerza Aerea Ecuatoriana, purchased 12 Meteor F.R.9s in 1954, and these equipped one of the three squadrons, or *escuadrillas*, of the Air Force's operational element. They remained in service for no less than 25 years, for it was not until 1979 that the six surviving F.R.9s were finally withdrawn from use; these Ecuadorean Meteors were the last of the type in operational service with any air arm, and outlived the Meteor in RAF operational service by no less than 17 years. Although small, with just 50 combat aircraft in 1983, the Fuerza Aerea Ecuatoriana is one of the most modern air forces in South America, with a first-line strength made up of Jaguar Internationals, Dassault Mirage F.1JE interceptors, Canberra B.6s and BAC Strikemaster Mk 89s, the most recent acquisition being ten Northrop F-5E fighters.

The Meteor P.R.10 was designed for longer range high altitude reconnaissance of a more strategic nature of the kind usually performed in the early post-war years by the Mosquito P.R.34. For better performance at high altitudes, it reverted to the original wing of 43 ft 0 in (13.1 m) span used on the Meteor F.III and earlier marks, and also featured the earlier tail unit of the F.III and F.IV. In addition to a nose camera installation very similar to the F.R.9's, additional vertical cameras were mounted in the rear fuselage and, unlike the F.R.9, the armament was deleted. The prototype P.R.10, VS968, made its first flight on 29 March 1950 and 58 of this mark were built in all, the last P.R.10, WH573, being

49

delivered to the RAF in April 1952.

The P.R.10 equipped one of the two home-based PR squadrons, No. 541 at Benson in Oxfordshire, in December 1950, replacing its Spitfire P.R.19s, and the following June No. 541 took its Meteors to Germany to reinforce the 2nd Tactical Air Force; it was based at Buckeburg and moved to Wunstorf in May 1957, being disbanded there on 6 September that year. No. 2 Sqn, also in Germany, had some Meteor P.R.10s on strength from March to June 1951 to supplement its F.R.9s. The P.R.10 began replacing the Mosquito P.R.34s of No. 13 Sqn at Fayid in the Canal Zone in January 1952, the squadron later moving to Abu Sueir and, in January 1956, to Akrotiri in Cyprus where, from May that year, Canberra P.R.7s began to replace the P.R.10s.

No. 81 Sqn at Tengah and Seletar, Singapore, which was the Far East Air Force's reconnaissance unit and was providing the vital photo recce coverage for operations against Communist terrorists in the jungle during the Malayan emergency, began to receive its first Meteor P.R.10s in December 1953 when it was still operating Spitfire P.R.19s and Mosquito P.R.34s. No. 81 had the unique distinction of making the RAF's last operational flights with these famous types, the last Spitfire sortie being flown on 1 April 1954 and the last by the Mosquito on 15 December 1955. The P.R.10s that replaced them remained in service until the last one was retired in July 1961, when re-equipment with the Canberra P.R.7, the first of which had arrived in 1958, was completed. No. 81 also operated some Pembroke C. (PR) 1s on air survey work from January 1956 to March 1958. The Meteor P.R.10 was really an interim type to provide a jet PR capability pending deliveries of the Canberra P.R.3 and 7.

As the first generation of British missiles reached the test firing and

Above left: One of the 12 Meteor F.R.9s purchased in 1954 by Ecuador's air force, the Fuerza Aerea Ecuatoriana.
Above right: The Meteor P.R.10, of which the prototype VS968 is seen here.

development stages in the latter half of the 1950s, the need arose for a target drone to provide a target as nearly as possible representative in terms of speed of the sort of aircraft these missiles would be likely to be used against. Some 200 Meteor F.4s and F.8s were converted into target drones with the designations U.15 and U.16 respectively, the design and conversion work being undertaken by Flight Refuelling Ltd at Tarrant Rushton airfield, Dorset. They were used both at the RAE Llanbedr in north Wales in conjunction with missile trials from Aberporth, being operated at Llanbedr by Short Bros & Harland Ltd, and at the Woomera Range in South and Western Australia, home of the Weapons Research Establishment.

Ninety-two Meteor F.4s were converted into U.15s and of these 59 were shipped out to Australia for use over the Woomera Range, being operated by the Target Aircraft Squadron of No. 1 AIRTU (Air Trials Unit) of the RAAF, which also operated Meteor U.16s, U.21s and U.21As; all the drone Meteors in Australia retained their RAF serials. Meteor U.15s arrived at the Bankstown, New South Wales, facility of the Fairey Aviation Co of Australasia Pty Ltd where they were prepared for handing over to the RAAF and were ferried to Fairey's Salisbury, South Australia, base for installation of the control and engagement equipment; the latter job was formerly done by the RAAF at Laverton, Victoria. The U.15 differed very little externally from the F.4 except for wing tip nacelles housing 35 mm cameras to record missile tracking of the U.15; these nacelles were jettisonable and recoverable for examination of the camera film after the aircraft had been hit by a missile.

The Meteor U.16, which entered service in 1960, had much smaller wing tip-mounted camera nacelles than the U.15 because they housed four each of the small-diameter very wide angle Type WRE No. 1 Mk 1 camera produced by the Fairey Aviation Co of Australasia. The U.16 also had a nose 30 in (0.76 m) longer than that of the Meteor F.8, and it contained an Elliott Type B.4 autopilot and command circuit gear; the U.16 was also fitted with command self-destruction equipment, and its internal fuel capacity was increased to 655 Imp gals (2,978 litres) by the addition of two tanks in the wings. At the 1961 SBAC Show Meteor U.16 WH505 was displayed in the static park, and featured transparent perspex panels in the nose where the cannon and ammunition bays formerly were, to reveal some of the automatic control equipment for display purposes. It still had its ejector seat fitted, and both the U.15 and U.16 could be flown by a pilot as well as by remote control, or as a radio-controlled aircraft carrying a pilot for checking the systems.

The U.16s were used mainly in the UK at Llanbedr, and in mid-1963 the 100th Meteor to be converted to a drone from an F.8, WK371, made its first piloted flight. Over 100 U.16 conversions had been made when production of Meteor drones ceased in 1963.

In 1961 work began on converting eight U.16s into the slightly more advanced U.21 – the variant for use at Woomera – the first of these flying as a U.21 on 31 May that year. Flight Refuelling Ltd also supplied kits for a further 15 U.16s to be modified to U.21 standard in Australia by the Fairey Aviation Co. In the end 10 U.21s and 14 of the very similar U.21A variant were used in Australia, and 10 U.16s had been shipped out there. The last Australian Meteor to be converted to a drone was U.21A A77-157.

The Night Fighters

One of the major mysteries of post-war RAF procurement policies is the length of time it took to recognise the need for a jet night fighter. Britain, which during the war could arguably be said to have led the world in such developments as AI radar (and especially in centimetric radars) allowed herself to fall behind in the early post-war years, so that it was not until 1951 that the first RAF squadrons re-equipped with Meteor N.F.11 and DH Vampire N.F.10 jet night fighters. The Mosquito N.F.36 equipped six home-based night fighter squadrons until replaced by Meteor N.F.11s and Vampire N.F.10s in 1951-52, but even then the new jets still had the same wartime AI Mk 10 radar and four 20-mm (.75-in) cannon armament as the Mosquito N.F.36. And this at a time when post-war developments embodied in the Avro Canada CF-100 Mk 4 and North American F-86D Sabre enabled these types to perform computerised collision-course interceptions directed by radar and autopilot with, instead of cannon (which could however be fitted to the CF-100), batteries of 2.75-in folding fin air-to-air rockets in wing tip pods and/or a retractable under-fuselage tray. Nor did the British jets have air-to-air missiles and even the Gloster Javelin, for which the Meteor N.F.11 to 14 served as an interim type, did not feature such missiles until its FAW. Mk 7 version was introduced with four DH Firestreaks under the wings in the late 1950s. By this time both the F-86D Sabre, which finally entered service in 1953 after numerous problems with its very advanced E-4 fire control system, and the CF-100 Mk 4, which

At least 33 Meteor N.F.11s were used for various trial installations and research jobs, like WD790 seen here, the RAF's last flying Meteor of this mark.

entered RCAF service the following year, had left Britain some way behind in the night and all-weather fighter field.

But within the limitations of its official Specification F.24/48, issued on 12 February 1949, the Meteor N.F.11 and the next three marks did a good job, and were exported to several countries. This Specification called for a night fighter version of the Meteor based on the T.7, to carry a pilot and navigator/radar operator in tandem, and to be suitable for a production run of 200 at a rate of 15 aircraft a month. AI Mk 10 radar was fitted in the extended nose, and this necessitated moving the four 20-mm (.75-in) Hispano Mk 5 cannon, with 640 rounds per gun, outboard to the wings, which were the original long span type of the Meteor F.III; a T.7-type cockpit canopy was featured and an F.8 tail unit, while the same RD.8 Derwent 8 engines as the F.8's were fitted. The specification also called for a gyro gunsight, vhf radio with a minimum of 16 channels, as well as IFF Mk 3GR and an AYF radio altimeter, while an alternative nose design for AI Mk 17 radar was called for in addition. Duration was to be at least two hours at 30,000 ft (9,144 m), and the specification demanded a much greater increase in longitudinal stability over previous marks.

Armstrong Whitworth was assigned responsibility for the design and production of the night fighter variants, and the Meteor N.F.11 prototype WA546 made its first flight on 31 May 1950, followed by the first production N.F.11, WD585, which first flew on 13 November that year; the Meteor T.7 VW413 was also test flown with the N.F.11's radar nose. Altogether 307 N.F.11s were built, and this variant first entered service with No. 29 Sqn at Tangmere in August 1951, where it replaced Mosquito N.F.30s. The N.F.11s served No. 29 until November 1957, when they were replaced by Javelin FAW.6s, although the squadron also had some Meteor N.F.12s from February to July 1958. Meteor N.F.11s equipped five more home-based night fighter squadrons (Nos. 85, 125, 141, 151 and 264) and four in Germany – No. 5 (formerly No. 68 Sqn), No. 11 (formerly No. 256 Sqn), Nos. 87 and 96 Squadrons – as well as a radar calibration unit, No. 527 Sqn, based at Warton, in which the N.F.11s were one of several types.

N.F.11s were also exported, 25 from RAF batches being supplied to the French Air Force, which also acquired two Meteor N.F.13s coded NF-F 364 and NF-F 365. As related in an earlier chapter, one of these N.F.11s, serialled NF11-3, was used to test the SFECMAS/Nord S.600 ramjet. Some N.F.11s were also supplied to the Belgian Air Force, replacing the Mosquito N.F.30s of Nos. 10 and 11

The Night Fighters

Squadrons at Beauvechain, and from 1957 the N.F.11s were themselves replaced by Avro Canada CF-100 Mk 5s. Twenty N.F.11s were also supplied to the Royal Danish Air Force, serialled 501-520, from November 1952 and they equipped *Eskadrille* 723, replacing the Meteor F.4s of that squadron; they served this unit until 1958 when they began to be replaced by F-86D Sabres, and six Danish N.F.11s were later converted to T.T.20 target tugs. Four N.F.11s were acquired by the Royal Australian Air Force, of which A77-3 (ex-WM262) delivered in August 1953, was used by the Aircraft Research and Development Unit; three more N.F.11s in Australian service retained their RAF serials WM372-374.

Several Meteor N.F.11s were used for various trial installations and experimental jobs, like WD745 which was used for some of the earliest test firings of the Fairey Fireflash air-to-air beam-riding missile in 1955-56; this had a proximity warhead and was the first British missile to destroy a target aircraft. It was used largely for training by the RAF until the DH Firestreak became available in quantity, and had two jettisonable solid propellant rocket boosters of 1,100-lb (500-kg) s.t. each to give a speed of about Mach 2. On the N.F.11 WD745, which had one ventral and two underwing tanks, the Fireflash was carried under each wing tip, the tips being squared off by a small cylindrical fairing with a short pylon at each end from which the Fireflash was suspended. The RAF's last flying Meteor N.F.11, WD 790 of the Royal Signals and Radar Establishment at Pershore, Worcestershire, and fitted with a new advanced radar in the nose, was displayed statically at the 1976 Greenham Common International Air Tattoo.

The N.F.11 was followed into production by the Meteor N.F.12 of which 100 were built, the first,

WS590, making its first flight on 21 April 1953. This mark differed from the N.F.11 in having improved APS-57 radar of US design in the lengthened nose. Meteor N.F.12s equipped nine home defence squadrons, and operated with N.F.14s in several of these. The Meteor N.F.13 was a 'tropicalised' version of the N.F.11 for use by Middle East Air Force squadrons, and 40 of this mark were built; the first, WM308, made its maiden flight on 23 December 1952. N.F.13s equipped two squadrons, No. 39 and No. 219; the former received N.F.13s to replace its Mosquito N.F.30s and 36s at Fayid in March 1953 to defend the Suez Canal Zone, and in January 1955 No. 39 moved to Luqa in Malta, remaining there until it was disbanded on 30 June 1958, still with Meteors. Also based in Egypt, at Kabrit, No. 219 Sqn received N.F.13s in April 1953 to replace its Mosquito N.F.36s and it flew them until disbanding on 1 September 1954, when the Meteors were flown back to the UK. The N.F.13 was also exported, six being supplied to the Syrian Air Force with serials 471-476, and another six went to the Egyptian Air Force, being serialled 1427-1432. The Israeli Air Force also took delivery of six N.F.13s during 1956-58, these having the quasi-military 'registrations' (denoting radio call signs) 4XFNA to 4XFNF for their delivery flights.

Last night fighter version was the Meteor N.F.14, which had a clear-view one-piece cockpit canopy designed by Armstrong Whitworth replacing the previous multi-framed one, and was 17 in (43 cm) longer than the previous night fighter marks. The first N.F.14, WS722, made its maiden flight on 23 October 1953 and altogether 100 of this mark were built, the last to be delivered being WS848 completed on 31 May 1954. Meteor N.F.14s equipped seven home defence squadrons, and also No. 60 Sqn of the Far East Air Force at Tengah, Singapore, which flew

them from October 1959 until they were replaced by Javelin FAW.9s in August 1961. No. 60 was in fact the last RAF Meteor squadron of all, and its N.F.14s were the last 'Meatboxes' of any kind in first-line service with the RAF. A number of N.F.14s were modified to the Meteor N.F.(T) 14 variant to give jet experience to navigators under training, and they were used for this purpose at Air Navigation Schools like No. 2 ANS at Stradishall, Suffolk; the N.F.(T) 14 had certain equipment differences from the N.F.14.

Altogether 547 of the night fighter marks were built, and three N.F.14s appeared on the British civil register. The first of these was G-ARCX (ex-WM261), registered to Ferranti Ltd in September 1960 for development work on airborne radars; this did not fly in civil marks until 21 January 1963, its Certificate of Airworthiness being issued on 8 February that year; it was withdrawn from use in February 1969. N.F.14 G-ASLW (ex-WS829) of Rolls-Royce Ltd was delivered to Hucknall on 13 September 1963 and its C of A was issued on 30 October that year; it previously served with No. 238 Operational Conversion Unit. In July 1969 it was acquired by the Blackbushe-based firm Target Towing Aircraft Co Ltd, headed by Mr Tony Osborne, and on 6 July that year left Hurn for Faro in Portugal, but some time later ditched in the Atlantic between Madeira and the Cape Verde Islands. It was officially cancelled as destroyed on 6 November 1969 at the same time as the pilot arrived, without his aircraft, in Lisbon. Target Towing Aircraft acquired a second N.F.14, G-AXNE (ex-WS804), and this was delivered to Blackbushe on 5 September 1969. The following day it left for Bordeaux via Exeter bearing the inscription 'Enterprise Films', and was reported in Senegal by 23 September, but shortly after it made an emergency landing at Bissau, Portuguese Guinea, and

was finally abandoned there.

Seventeen N.F.11s were converted into Meteor T.T.20 target tugs by Armstrong-Whitworth between December 1957 and February 1965; this variant had an ML Type G wind-driven winch mounted on a pylon on the starboard wing centre section, and provision for carrying in the rear fuselage in containers four high-speed radar-reflective sleeve targets, which were streamed automatically. A winch operator in the rear cockpit controlled target streaming or winching in, and a Rushton target resembling a small air-to-air missile could also be towed. The T.T.20 was first ordered by the Royal Navy, and some later saw service with the RAF. Later the Navy's target towing and radar calibration requirements for warships in home waters were provided under contract to the Admiralty by the Airwork Services Ltd Fleet Requirements Unit at Hurn airport, near Bournemouth, using civilian pilots to fly Navy

aircraft. By 1962 these numbered five Meteor T.T.20s, WD610, WD649, WD657, WM159 and WM292, and 14 Sea Hawk FB.5s and FGA.6s, plus a Meteor T.7 WL350, and three Sea Fury FB.11s. A very similar function was performed by No. 3 Civilian Anti-Aircraft Co-Operation Unit, operated by Exeter Airport Ltd under contract to the Air Ministry, which in 1963 was using five Meteor T.T.20s and seven Mosquito T.T.35s for target towing for the Royal Navy and Army units mainly in the south and south-west of England, and also 16 Vampire T.11s for tactical exercises with, and providing anti-aircraft training for, Army and Territorial Army units. Again, these aircraft were flown and maintained by civilians, although in RAF markings, and in 1970 No. 3 CAACU moved its operations from Exeter to St Mawgan. Some T.T.20s were still in RAF use with No. 1574 Flight at Changi, Singapore, as late as 1968.

Also converted to T.T.20s in 1959 were six Royal Danish Air Force

The Meteor N.F.12 differed from the N.F.11 in having the improved Westinghouse APS-57 radar (British designation AI Mk 21) in a longer and cleaner nose. N.F.11 WD782 tested a dummy APS-57 nose, and WD687 tested the N.F.12's fin which had extra area in the shape of small leading edge fillets fairing into the tailplane bullet.

Meteor N.F.11s, serialled 504, 508, 512 and 517 to 519. In early 1962 Svensk Flygtjänst AB was awarded a three-year contract to carry out target towing for the Danish armed forces, and it acquired four of the Danish T.T.20s on lease from the Danish Government, these taking up Swedish civil registrations in the autumn of 1962. Thus T.T.20 512 became SE-DCF, T.T.20 517 became SE-DCG, T.T.20 508 became SE-DCH and 519 became SE-DCI.

Meteor production of all marks totalled 3,947 aircraft, including 547 night fighters built by Armstrong-Whitworth and 480 F.8s built in Belgium and Holland.

Preserved Meteors in the UK

F.9/40 first prototype DG202/G at RAF Cosford Aerospace Museum.

Meteor F.3 EE416 – used for Martin-Baker ejector seat trials: nose section is in the Science Museum, South Kensington, London.

Meteor F.4 EE531 (7090M) at Midland Aircraft Museum, Baginton, near Coventry.

Meteor F.4 EE549 (7008M), World Speed Record breaker, is at the RAF Museum, Hendon.

Meteor F.4 VT229 (7151M) at Duxford, Cambridgeshire.

Meteor F.8 VZ462:E with outer wings of T.T.20 WM234, with World War II Preservation Society at Lasham, Hampshire.

Meteor T.T.8 VZ467:01 with 1TWU at Brawdy, Wales.

Meteor F.8 VZ477 (7741M): 'gate guardian' at 5 Radar HQ, Bristol.

Meteor F.8 VZ530's wings with World War II Preservation Society, Lasham, Hampshire.

Meteor F.R.9 VZ608 with RB.108 lift engine at Newark Air Museum, Winthorpe.

Meteor T.7 VZ638:X at Southend Air Museum, Essex.

Meteor T.7 WA591 (7917M) at RAF St Athan Museum.

Meteor T.7/8 WA634, used by Martin-Baker for zero-level ejector seat trials, is at RAF St Athan Museum.

Meteor T.7 WA638, used by Martin-Baker at Chalgrove for ejection tests.

Meteor T.7 WA662 with RAE Llanbedr.

Meteor T.7 WA669 at RAF Leeming, Yorkshire, as one of the 'Vintage Pair'.

Meteor T.T.20 WD646:R (8189M), of 2030 Sqn Air Training Corps, is displayed at Sheldon TAVR Centre.

Meteor N.F.11 WD686 at Duxford, Cambridgeshire.

Meteor N.F.11 WD790 used by the RSRE at Pershore to test new AI radar.

Meteor F.8 WE925 at the Wales Aircraft Museum, Cardiff.

Meteor F.8 WF643:X at Norfolk and Suffolk Aviation Museum, Flixton, Suffolk.

Meteor T.7 WF784 (7895M): 'gate guardian' at Quedgely.

Meteor T.7 WF791 at RAF Leeming, Yorkshire, as one of the 'Vintage Pair'.

Meteor T.7 WF825:Z with 2491 ATC Sqn at RAF Lyneham, Wiltshire.

Meteor T.7 WF877, used for ejector seat trials, is at Torbay Aircraft Museum, Higher Blagdon, Devon.

Meteor T.7 WH132 (7906M) with 276 ATC Sqn at Chelmsford.

Meteor T.7 WH166: 'gate guardian' at RAF Digby, Lincolnshire.

Meteor F.8 WH291 with World War II Preservation Society, Lasham, Hampshire.

Meteor F.8 WH301 (7930M) at RAF Museum, Hendon.

Meteor U.16 WH320:N with RAE Llanbedr.

Meteor F.8 WH364: 'gate guardian' at RAF Kemble.

Meteor U.16 WH453:L with RAE Llanbedr.

Meteor F.8 WH456 (7750M), painted as WL168, at RAF Swinderby, Lincolnshire.

Meteor F.8 WK654: 'gate guardian' at Neatishead.

Meteor U.16 WK800:Z with RAE Llanbedr.

Meteor F.8 WK935 (7869M) with prone pilot nose at RAF Cosford Aerospace Museum.

Meteor F.8 WK968: 'gate guardian' at RAF Odiham, Hampshire.

Meteor F.8 WK991, in 56 Sqn markings, at Duxford, Cambridgeshire.

Meteor F.8 WL181's rear fuselage and cockpit with the North East Aircraft Museum at Usworth.

Meteor T.7 WL332 with the Wales Aircraft Museum at Cardiff.

Meteor T.7 WL345: mounted on a pylon in a garage forecourt near Hastings, East Sussex.

Meteor T.7 WL349: 'gate guardian' at Staverton.

Meteor T.7 WL360: 'gate guardian' at RAF Locking, Somerset.

Meteor T.7 WL405 with the RAE Apprentice School at Farnborough.

Meteor T.7 WL419 used for spares for T.7 WA638 by Martin-Baker at Chalgrove.

Meteor T.T.20 WM167 with Douglas Arnold Collection at Blackbushe. Now registered G-LOSM to Brencham Historic Aircraft Co Ltd of Hurn.

Meteor T.T.20 WM224: displayed at the Kings Head public house at High Road, North Weald, Essex.

Meteor T.T.20 WM234's centre section with North East Aircraft Museum, Usworth.

Meteor T.T.20 WM292:841 at FAA Museum at Yeovilton, Somerset.

Meteor T.7 WS103: 'gate guardian' at Wroughton.

Meteor N.F.12 WS692 (7605M) with the Technical Block at Cranwell, Bedfordshire.

Meteor N.T.(T)14 WS726:G (7960M) with 1855 Sqn ATC at Royton, near Oldham, Lancashire.

Meteor N.F.(T)14 WS739 (7961M) with South Yorkshire Aircraft Preservation Society at Misson.

Meteor N.F.(T)14 WS760 (7964M) at Duxford, Cambridgeshire.

Meteor N.F.(T)14 WS774 (7959M): 'gate guardian' at Ely RAF Hospital.

Meteor N.F14 WS776 (7716M): 'gate guardian' at RAF North Luffenham.

Meteor N.F.(T)14 WS788 (7967M): 'gate guardian' at RAF Leeming, Yorkshire.

Meteor N.F.(T)14 WS792 (7965M): 'gate guardian' at Carlisle.

Meteor N.F.14 WS807: 'gate guardian' at Eastern Radar, Watton.

Meteor N.F.14 WS832:W with Solway Firth Preservation Society, Scotland.

Meteor N.F.14 WS838 at RAF Cosford Aerospace Museum.

Meteor N.F.14 (T) WS843 (7937M) at RAF St Athan Museum.

Meteor N.F.13 4X-FNA, ex-Israeli Air Force, with World War II Preservation Society at Lasham, Hampshire.

Note: some preserved Meteors have, as well as the normal serials, Maintenance serials ending in 'M', but these are not always carried.

Gloster Meteor
technical description

Type: twin-engined day, night and all-weather fighter, jet trainer, photo reconnaissance aircraft, target drone and target tug.

Wings: Two-spar stressed skin wings divided into a centre section and two outer panels. Wing section EC1240 for centre section and roots of outer panels, tapering to EC1040 at wing tips. Spars in centre section are spaced by six major ribs interspersed with lighter skin ribs. Engine nacelles are built up between the inner and outer nacelle ribs at each side (between which each engine is mounted) and are based on two main frames attached to the spars. 'Banjo'-type rear spar enables the jet pipe to pass through it; spar webs and booms are of steel in the jet pipe area. Complete top half of nacelle between the spars is detachable for accessibility to the engine; also detachable is entire nose of cowling forward of the front spar. Undercarriage bays inboard of the nacelles between the spars. Hydraulically-operated split flaps and air brakes, the latter above and below the centre section on each side. Outer wings attached by pin joints at the front and rear spars. Detachable wing tips. Internally mass-balanced all-metal ailerons with long chord geared tabs; spring tabs on later production Meteor F.8s.

Fuselage: All-metal stressed skin fuselage structure divided into three main units – the front fuselage with nosewheel assembly, the centre fuselage integral with the wing centre section and engine nacelles, and the rear fuselage. Basis of the front fuselage structure is two vertical webs and three solid bulkheads; the nose bulkhead forms the front wall of the pressure cabin, the seat bulkhead forming the rear wall, the front spar bulkhead completing the rear end of the front fuselage. Front fuselage is joined to the centre fuselage at four longeron joints. The front and rear spar bulkheads form the boundaries of the centre fuel tank bay; there are two quickly detachable tank doors in the top of it. The semi-monocoque rear fuselage, like the front fuselage, is attached to the centre at four longeron joints, and has Z-section frames and top-hat section stringers. The last two frames are extended upwards to form the lower fin posts, and provide attachment points for the tailplane and upper fin.

Tail Unit: All-metal stressed skin tail unit; the rudder is split by the tailplane into two halves which are joined by a tubular spar, and the two elevators are joined in a similar manner. Mass- and aerodynamically-balanced rudder and elevators. Adjustable trim tab in lower portion of rudder, and a similar tab in

each elevator; the rudder tab also acts as a balance tab. 'Bullet' fairing at the tailplane/fin junction (this was not fitted on the F.9/40 prototypes).

Landing Gear: Nosewheel retracts rearwards and is enclosed by three doors. Main wheels retract inwards into bays in centre section, and have shortening device to lessen the space they occupy when retracted; each main leg is enclosed by two doors. All three undercarriage units employ the Dowty levered suspension principle pioneered in the Gloster E.28/39. Hydraulic retraction, with a hand pump for emergency extension of undercarriage and flaps if hydraulics fail. Dunlop pneumatically-operated main wheel brakes. Nosewheel is castoring and self-centring.

Power Plants and Fuel System: The F.9/40 prototypes had various engines (see text). The Meteor F.I and the first 15 F.IIIs had the 1,700-lb (771-kg) s.t. Rolls-Royce Welland I centrifugal flow turbojets. Remaining F.IIIs had the 2,000-lb (910-kg) s.t. RB.37 Derwent I centrifugal flow turbojets, and the Meteor F.IV, T.7 and U.15 had 3,500-lb (1,585-kg) s.t. Derwent 5 engines. The F.8 and subsequent marks, as well as later production T.7s, had the 3,600-lb (1,633-kg) s.t. Derwent 8 jets. Centre fuselage contains a two-cell self-sealing 325-Imp gal (1,480-litres) fuel tank on Meteor F.III and F.IV; on F.8 a 30-in (76-cm) forward fuselage extension houses a second tank of 95 Imp gals (432 litres). One 180-Imp gal (818-litres) ventral drop tank and two 100-Imp gal (455-litres) underwing drop tanks can be carried; on later production F.IVs the underwing tanks were fitted for ferry flights only.

Accommodation: Fully pressurised pilot's cockpit with heating, ventilating, anti-icing and demisting systems; normal spade grip control column. Full cabin pressure differential of 3-lb/sq in is achieved at 24,000 ft (7,315 m). Jettisonable sliding cockpit hood; sideways-opening hood on Meteor F.I, T.7, N.F.11 to 14 and T.T.20. Windscreen consists of three bullet-proof panels. Martin-Baker Mk IE ejector seat in Meteor F.8, F.R.9 and P.R.10; this seat was later modified to Mk 2E standard for automatic separation of pilot from seat in high altitude ejections, and Mk 2E seats were later still fitted with the Duplex drogue system for safe ejections down to 125 ft (38 m).

Meteor T.7 has pilot and pupil seated in tandem with full dual controls, and provision for fitting amber screens in the cockpit for instrument training. The Meteor N.F.11 to 14 seat pilot and navigator/radar operator, the latter being replaced by a winch operator in the T.T.20 target tug conversion.

Armament: Four 20-mm British Hispano Mk 5 cannon mounted two on each side

of the cockpit between the main fuselage diaphragms and outer skin, and accessible through large gun doors. Cannon heating and pneumatic ground cocking systems; to operate the latter and also the main wheel brakes the F.IV had a Heywood compressor in the rear fuselage charging an air bottle, while the F.I and F.III had two ground-charged compressed air bottles. Ammunition fed via Mk I or Mk V belt feed systems, the cartridge cases and links being ejected (on the F.IV and later variants) through small chutes in lower fuselage skin. Gyro gunsight for the pilot. G.45B cine camera gun in fuselage nose. The Meteor N.F.11 to 14 had the Hispano Mk 5 cannon, with 640 rounds per gun, moved outboard to the wings.

Most RAF Meteors did not carry external 'stores', although the F.8 could have attachment points for two 1,000-lb (454-kg) bombs or eight 95-lb (43-kg) rocket projectiles. Some exported Meteors, like the F.8s of the RAAF's No. 77 Sqn in Korea (see text) carried external 'stores'; Israeli Air Force F.8s could take four American HVAR rocket projectiles under each wing.

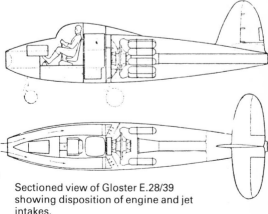

This sectional diagram of the Whittle W.2B which was developed into the Rolls-Royce Welland shows the basic centrifugal flow layout with guide vanes in the compressor intakes, and the original 'return flow' combustion chambers.

Sectioned view of Gloster E.28/39 showing disposition of engine and jet intakes.

Specifications

Meteor Performance

F.4
Max Level Speed	585 mph (940 km/h) at sea level
Max Speed at 30,000 ft (9,144 m)	540 mph (870 km/h) (Mach 0.81)
Max Rate of Climb at Sea Level	7,500 ft/min (2,286 m/min)
Max Rate of Climb at 30,000 ft (9,144 m)	3,300 ft/min (1,006 m/min)
Time to 30,000 ft (9,144 m) (clean)	5 minutes
Absolute Ceiling	49,000 ft (14,935 m)
Range (clean)	420 miles (676 km) at 30,000 ft (9,144 m)
Range with ventral and underwing tanks	1,000 miles (1,610 km)
Take-off run to clear 50 ft (15.25 m)	834 yards (762 m)
Landing run from 50 ft (15.25 m)	1,000 yards (914 m)

F.8
Max Level Speed	592 mph (952 km/h) (Mach 0.78) at sea level
Max Speed at 30,000 ft (9,144 m)	550 mph (885 km/h)
Max Rate of Climb at Sea Level	7,000 ft/min (2,134 m/min)
Max Rate of Climb at 30,000 ft (9,144 m)	2,700 ft/min (823 m/min)
Time to 30,000 ft (9,144 m) (clean)	6.5 minutes
Range (clean)	690 miles (1,110 km) at 40,000 ft (12,192 m)
Range with ventral and underwing tanks	1,200 miles (1,931 km)
Take-off run to clear 50 ft (15.25 m)	480 yards (439 m)
Landing run from 50 ft (15.25 m)	510 yards (466 m)

T.7
Max Level Speed	585 mph (940 km/h) at sea level
Max Speed at 30,000 ft (9,144 m)	540 mph (870 km/h) (Mach 0.81)
Max Rate of Climb at Sea Level	8,000 ft/min (2,440 m/min)
Max Rate of Climb at 30,000 ft (9,144 m)	3,650 ft/min (1,110 m/min)
Time to 30,000 ft (9,144 m) (clean)	6.5 minutes
Range (clean)	470 miles (756 km) at 30,000 ft (9,144 m)
Range with ventral and underwing tanks	1,000 miles (1,610 km)
Take-off run to clear 50 ft (15.25 m)	785 yards (720 m)
Landing run from 50 ft (15.25 m)	935 yards (855 m)

N.F.14
Max Level Speed	576 mph (927 km/h)
Max Rate of Climb at Sea Level	5,800 ft/min (1,768 m/min)
Range (clean)	795 miles (1,280 km)

Meteor Production

F.9/40 prototypes: eight built (DG202-DG209); four more cancelled (DG210-DG213).

Meteor F.I: 20 built (EE210-EE229).

F.II: proposed DH Goblin-engined version of F.I not built.

F.III: 280 built; the first 15 (EE230-EE244) had Welland I turbojets.

F.IV: 657 built, of which 45 (including seven for the Egyptian Air Force) were constructed by Armstrong Whitworth.

P.R.V: One, VT347, converted from F.IV.

F.VI: not built.

T.7: 712 built.

F.8: 1,183 built, including 430 by Armstrong Whitworth, and 480 built in Holland and Belgium by Fokker and Avions Fairey SA.

F.R.9: 126 built.

P.R.10: 58 built.

N.F.11: 307 built

N.F.12: 100 built

N.F.13: 40 built

N.F.14: 100 built

U.15: 92 converted into target drones from F.4s by Flight Refuelling Ltd.

U.16: over 100 converted from F.8s by Flight Refuelling Ltd.

U.21, U.21A: ten U.21s and 14 U.21As converted from U.16s for use in Australia.

T.T.20: 17 target tug conversions of N.F.11 for RAF and RN plus six for Royal Danish Air Force.

Dimensions

Span: 37 ft 2 in (11.33 m)
Span (F.I, F.III, Mks 10-14): 43 ft (13.1 m)
Length (F.I, F.III, F.4): 41 ft 4 in (12.6 m)
Length (T.7, F.R.9): 43 ft 6 in (13.25 m)
Length (F.8): 44 ft 7 in (13.59 m)
Length (N.F.11 to 13): 48 ft 6 in (14.78 m)
Length (N.F.14): 49 ft 11½ in (15.23 m)
Height (F.I to T.7 and P.R.10): 13 ft (3.96 m)
Height (Mks 8, 9 and 11-14): 13 ft 10 in (4.22 m)
Wing Area (gross): 350 sq ft (32.5 m²) with 37 ft 2 in (11.33 m) span wings.
Aspect Ratio: 3.9 with 37 ft 2 in (11.33 m) span wings.

Meteor Weights

F.4
Empty	10,050 lb (4,559 kg)
Loaded (with full internal fuel):	15,000 lb (6,800 kg)
Wing loading:	41.4 lb/sq ft (202 kg/m²)

F.8
Empty	10,626 lb (4,820 kg)
Loaded (with full internal fuel):	19,100 lb (8,664 kg)
Wing loading:	45 lb/sq ft

T.7
Empty	10,540 lb (4,780 kg)
Loaded (with full internal fuel):	14,000 lb (6,350 kg)

N.F.11
Empty	about 11,900 lb (5,400 kg)
Loaded (with full internal fuel):	22,000 lb (9,979 kg)

Acknowledgements

The author would particularly like to thank Derek N. James, formerly of the Gloster Aircraft Co Ltd, for providing many of the black-and-white photographs for this book, and Stuart Howe of the RAF Museum, Hendon, for supplying many of the colour photos. Grateful acknowledgements are also due to the following sources for illustrations:

Air-Britain: 39 (bottom), slides 21 (top), 18 (bottom), 24 (top) and S21
Charles W. Cain: 47, 48
P.M. Corbell: slide 24 (centre)
J.J. Halley: slides S10, 18 (top), 21 (centre) and S22
Stuart Howe: 4, 8, 9 (top), 9 (bottom), 33, 35, 39 (top), 40 (all), 46, 51
pp. 17, 20 (top), 20 (bottom), 22/23, 22 (inset) and 23
Derek N. James/Gloster Aircraft: 12, 25, 26 (inset), 31, 34, 36, 37, 44, 45 (left), 45 (right), 49, 50 (both)
Martin-Baker Aircraft Co Ltd: 27 (inset), 26/27
T. Mason: slide S14
A. Reinhard: slides S11, S12
Rolls-Royce Ltd: 16, 41 (both), 42, 43 (bottom)
R. Shadbolt: slide 21 (bottom)
F. Willemsen: slide 24 (bottom)